The Non-Techie Guide to Enterprise Software

Buying, Implementing, and Understanding the

Enterprise Software Process

Perry Harris

The Non-Techie Guide to Enterprise Software

Buying, Implementing, and Understanding the Enterprise Software Process

By Perry Harris

Published by Rapid River Press

All inquiries should be directed to: NonTechieGuide@outlook.com

Library of Congress Cataloging-in-Publication Data

Harris, Perry

      The Non-Techie Guide to Enterprise Software / Perry Harris

      ISBN: 978-0-9989511-0-2 (paperback)

      1. Computer software industry.   2. Technology consultants.

      3. Application software--Software.   4. Sales.

Table of Contents

i

What's This Book About?

Your ego tells you that you have a lot of useful stuff in your head and that maybe you should assemble that information into a book. I searched for existing books on enterprise software and most were focused on how to architect/code software and not on the business/implementation side of enterprise software.

I didn't want to write a completely stuffy and boring business book because that would be well … boring. I own and enjoy a bunch of books that I would classify as 'bathroom readers' because they are constructed to allow you to spend a few minutes reading something interesting or funny and then you can move along. So, I hatched the idea of making the book a bit of a hybrid: part business book and part bathroom reader to hopefully make an arguably dry topic a bit more fun and interesting.

I've worked on many different types of enterprise software projects over the last 25 years. I've seen a bunch that have been really well done and I've seen a few disasters. Most of them fall somewhere in between – some pain but ultimately, they got done. If you sit down and think about what has made the good ones good, and the bad ones bad, you start to see patterns. That's what this book is about – describing all the pieces and parts that go into enterprise software projects and talking about them in a way that will allow you to apply them to your projects and be more successful.

In 1999, I founded Varden Technologies because I wanted to build a software consulting/integration firm that was great at implementing enterprise software for the financial services industry. I have repeatedly said to my co-workers: 'when I write my book, this is going in it'. Well – here it is, all the stories, anecdotes, mistakes, and assorted other stuff that I guess all rolls up to the term 'Experience'.

Am I qualified to write this? I'll give you a quick rundown of my background and leave it to you to decide:

- I've worked in the financial services world for about 30 years. I started out in custodian bank operations (yuck) and learned a lot of things that I thought were useless at the time, but years later realize I learned a lot of important nuts and bolts of the financial services industry.

- I've held several roles as product manager, director of professional services, and vice president of client services for several large international investment technology/software firms.

- I'm the founder and former President/CEO of Varden Technologies. Varden was a software and consulting firm focused in the investment management industry. The company was started with a laptop and an idea and over 15 years we sold and delivered more than $60 million in software and related consulting services and established ourselves as a market leader in the client communications software market. I managed to keep it in business through two crappy stock market cycles so I will give myself a little credit and call it more than luck. I sold the firm in 2015 which has given me time to finish the book!

- I have a hands-on database and programming background – so yes, I have some technical skills (the real technical guys that I work with think I'm just a sales guy so I guess the term technical is relative).

- I have a BA in Economics from Boston University and an MBA from the Babson - F.W. Olin School of Business. I think what is important is that I do not have a formal technical education – more on that later.

I've seen many sides of the enterprise software world. We'll talk about the different players in enterprise software later but I've been almost all of them at one point or another in my career which hopefully gives me a unique perspective on the big picture.

As you can see from the bullets above, my background is primarily in the financial services industry. Although most of the book is based on many experiences in financial services, I have been involved with and talked with colleagues in other verticals and the principles discussed are applicable to a wide range of industries.

Someone asked me if I thought that I was giving away too many software vendor 'secrets' in this book. Sort of an interesting question and my response is: a.) I have addressed topics that I think are productive for both vendor and buyers to have a better understanding of the motivations of each party, and b.) there are still plenty of secrets. It's like a book on fishing – I can teach you about techniques and tides but I'm not going to give away all my spots.

I was also asked if I wrote the book for readers from software buyers or vendors. It's for both – I didn't feel like I needed to pick a side. Sometimes I'm talking about the buyers and other times about the vendors. Confusing? I don't think so – you will work it out.

Software is an interesting and complex business that I am fortunate to have stumbled into as a career and even though my kids make fun of me for doing something that 'nobody really understands', I'd pick it again.

The One Who Speaks of Floppy Disks

Konica Minolta[1] did a commercial several years back where a bunch of youthful workers are talking at the photocopier about things they had to do in the 'old days' when in walks the Elder – 'the one who speaks of floppy disks'. It is on YouTube and a great investment of 31 seconds. I bring it up because a.) it's funny, and b.) I have become that guy.

The Elder shakes his head and says: 'you're all soft' and walks away. I might make a little fun of terms, people, and some of the new ways of doing things – I just can't help myself.

Additionally, if you are too young for my 80's references (or earlier), I encourage you to spend some time looking at the references section at the end of the book. I'm told that the 80's are cool again (were they ever not?). So, read the books, listen to the music, and watch the movies, commercials, and TV shows – it is a solid collection and all pretty accessible on the web.

Who Should Read It?

First and foremost, the book is written for non-technical people in a way that is hopefully not tech-intimidating. I wanted to cover the basics for those new to the topic but believe there are also many tidbits and perspectives that will be insightful for the jaded, grizzled veteran as well. I have tried to write the book in an informal, conversational way but this may just be an excuse for my inability to use proper grammar. I'm sure some techies will not agree with how I describe, characterize, or oversimplify certain things and that is fine – they are welcome to write their own books.

You should read (and tell all your friends to read!) if you fit in below:

- Any C-Level Executive or Manager who works with an IT department or relies on enterprise software to run their business.

- People involved in enterprise software implementations.

- Folks in the software sales process.

- Candidates new to the field who are considering a career in the space or someone looking to change careers into this area.

- Anyone who finds it in the bathroom and has a little time to kill.

Acknowledgements

This book is dedicated to:

My father – a great entrepreneurial role model. It is no accident that all five of his children have been successful running their own businesses. He has taught us all the value of integrity and not being afraid to take risks. I have met a lot of his former co-workers and colleagues over the years and many of them have said to me that he is one of the smartest people they have ever met. I think humility may keep him from agreeing to being one of the smartest, but I think he would concede that he does things the right way, treats people well, and knows how to get to the core of a problem – maybe that combination is what makes him so smart. Thank you for showing us the way.

Special thanks to:

Deb and Alex for grinding through early versions of the book – your feedback undoubtedly made the overall result better.

My wife Patti for the million things that you do for me but specifically assisting with editing, layout, and ultimately helping to push it over the finish line.

How the Book is Organized

A few pages earlier I described the book as a hybrid of a business and a bathroom book. There are traditional chapters to the book, but mixed in you will find standalone topics designed to help break things up a bit and create short, readable chunks. These topics can be somewhat more opinionated and possibly random but managed to make their way into the final cut of the book. Maybe you intended to read the whole book but find yourself just glassing over – it's ok. Just focus on the colored/boxed sections and skip the heavier stuff. These items will be found in boxes such as below:

> **Opinion, Essay, or Travel Related**
>
> Something (hopefully) insightful or interesting ...

For the color-blind readers, as well as anyone reading a black/white version, there are also icons to help classify the topics:

Glossary of Terms

Career/Personnel

Business Topic

Vendor Related (Get it? It's a hotdog vendor truck)

Fun – Generally related to food, travel, or some random topic

🐘 Parading Elephants (A Very Short Story)

Early in my career, I was working as a business analyst and was assigned to work with my firm's sales team to define, scope, and price a large accounting system sale/implementation. We spent months defining requirements, working with the prospective client, and ended up back in a conference room putting together the proposal. We broke everything down, added up the costs and it came out to about 6 million dollars.

The following week we travel to the prospective client's office to present our proposal. The sales guy who owns the deal spends an hour presenting our approach, etc. and then at the end of the meeting we get to the last page of the proposal, which provides a breakdown of all the costs (the cost is always on the last page). The total at the bottom of the deal sheet is $8.5 million. I'm a junior guy on the project so I don't say a thing, but I'm wondering if it is a mistake. The meeting wraps up and later in the hallway I ask the sales guy why the numbers were so different. "Perry, we're going to parade a few elephants by their door while they aren't really looking." I'm sorry but I really don't understand. "They have the money and there are a bunch of things that we want to do with the project so we have worked some additional things into the proposal."

Oh.

Thus began my enterprise software journey. I've seen and learned a lot of things since then, so here we go …

Chapter 1: Enterprise Software – Getting Started

This section may not be particularly interesting to those already familiar with enterprise software. It is written for those new to the topic to provide some basic understanding and an overview of things before I roll into more specifics in the rest of the book.

Enterprise Software Defined

What makes enterprise software special? How is it different from 'regular' software? You can probably use "the Google"* to find a nice academic answer but generally, enterprise software has one or more of the following characteristics:

- **Expensive** – The amount spent is relative to the organization, however, usually enough money is being allocated that the project is approved at a high level in the organization. Early in my career, someone told me that what qualifies a software system as 'enterprise' is software you can be fired over if the project is a

---

* President George W. Bush famously referred to Google Search as 'the Google' in 2006. From Google's trademark rules site, this is incorrect and you should follow the below guidelines: Use the trademark only as an adjective, never as a noun or verb, and never in the plural or possessive form. Use the generic term for the product following the trademark, for example: Google search engine, Google search, Google web search.

failure. At the time, I thought it was funny but 20 years later realize that it was pretty accurate.

- **Multi-user** – Multiple people are using the application at the same time. It is being used across the E-N-T-E-R-P-R-I-S-E. Ah, 'used across the enterprise' – I bet that's where the name came from.

- **Interfaces/Integration** – Often the system will interface or exchange information with other software systems.

- **Underlying database** – Usually enterprise software systems store a bunch of data for the enterprise such as sales info, orders, inventory, etc.

- **High volumes** – With lots of users on the system doing different things at the same time, how does the system perform? Does the system become slow; do different users step on one another's work? Enterprise systems (should) be architected to address these issues.

- **Relies on infrastructure** – Generally utilizes some server infrastructure that has backup or failover capabilities, so more complex than running on your laptop.

Aside from the bullets above, one of the key things about enterprise software is that it needs to be implemented. An implementation consists of all the planning, business re-engineering, integration, testing, training, and rollout associated with the new product. Changing an organization's enterprise CRM, accounting system, inventory system, etc. is generally disruptive, time consuming, and expensive. We are going to talk a lot about the implementation cycle and how it can be approached effectively. Also, you will see the terms software system, solution, and application used interchangeably throughout the book.

Firms decide to buy an enterprise software system for many reasons but the primary drivers are:

- Make us more efficient (spend less dollars)

- Increase sales (collect more dollars)

- Make better business decisions

- Improve quality / consistency

- Eliminate outdated technology or manual processes

I've seen many firms go through cost/benefit analysis, return on investment, risk analysis, etc. I have also seen firms buy a system because they want to be able to tell their clients that they have one or because the decision maker is friends with the owner of the software company. Regardless of how or why the system is picked, it needs to go through the long adventure of selection through go-live, so that is what we are going to talk about.

> *What qualifies a software system as 'enterprise' is software you can be fired over if the project is a failure.*

The Players

I refer to these different roles throughout the book so thought it would be helpful to define them a bit up front for those new to the topic. It's like when you read an epic fantasy book like the Hobbit[2] or Game of Thrones[3] – they give you a tally of the characters up front (and usually a map of the fictitious world too, but I'm not doing the map part).

Vendors (Software Providers)

A software vendor develops and sells software, provides software-as-a service (SAAS), and/or offers software-related services. Vendors can be small boutique organizations who offer a single solution or a large organization that offers a wide variety of products and services.

Client (Prospective Client, Prospect)

A client is a firm that has contracted with a vendor to license and/or implement a software solution. A prospective client is a firm that is evaluating purchasing software from one or more software vendors.

Consultants (Third-Party Consultants)

For the purposes of our discussion, a consultant is any third-party resource that is hired to work on our project to assist with the selection or implementation of a software application. I am drawing a distinction between consultants who work at the software vendor (most vendors have consulting/implementation teams) and other consultants.

Business Analyst (BA)

A business analyst is typically responsible for analyzing business data, processes, and workflow associated with the software in question. Business analysts often get involved in the testing phase of the project and can often be responsible for writing test plans, performing test plans, and providing end-user training. A lot of things can get dumped into the business analyst bucket and BAs are often the non-technical doers of many tasks on a project.

Quality Assurance (QA)

QA staff are responsible for the testing of a software application. Software firms typically have dedicated QA teams who are responsible for finding and recreating software bugs/defects. The developers (see below) are responsible for repairing the bugs and the QA team will retest with the goal of releasing a new version of the software with fixes.

Larger software clients may have their own dedicated testing team, particularly if they do a lot of custom development. However, in many shops the testing responsibility falls to the business analyst and operation teams.

Project Managers (PM)

The project manager is responsible for managing the overall progress of a software project. There can be PMs assigned by both the vendor and the client to manage the process. The project manager(s) typically manages the project plan/schedule, budget, and facilitates team resources and communication.

Developers (Programmers, Software Engineers)

Developers are responsible for writing the code that makes up the software application or provides data integration of the software to other systems. Developers can come from the vendor, the client, or from third-party consultants.

Users (End Users, Business Users)

Users are the people who will use the software in question to perform a business function. If it is an Accounting system, there will be accountants, auditors, etc. who will all be users of the system. For a Customer Relationship Management (CRM) system, the users would be the sales team, management, etc.

Systems Infrastructure (Sys Admin)

I'm grouping all the technology infrastructure people who deal with networks, servers, databases, and desktop support into this bucket. They generally work behind the scenes but are responsible for keeping everything running – unsung heroes in the overall scheme of things. Sorry for lumping you all together.

Procurement

Large clients often have a group that is responsible for the procurement of software, services, and stuff that the client needs to run their business. Procurement is often responsible for negotiating prices with the vendors and working to get the best deal for the client. For clients without a procurement group, the project manager or business sponsor is typically responsible for the negotiation and completion of the agreement.

Project Sponsor

The project sponsor is the individual(s) at the client who is championing and/or funding the new software solution. Vendors look to identify this person as they view him as the ultimate decision maker/check writer at the client.

The Enterprise Software Process

Before digging into the details, here is a quick rundown of the key elements of the enterprise software process and the key topics that we are going to cover in the rest of the book.

- **Software Search** – Your firm has decided to get some new software – you need to select a system.

- **Contract** – Once you select your system, you need to agree to financial terms and sign an agreement to use the software.

- **Implementation** – Enterprise software needs to be implemented which consists of all the integration, workflow, and the million other tasks that need to be performed before you start using it.

- **Go-Live** – Once the implementation cycle is complete, you are ready to cut over to the new system.

- **Post-Live** – Congratulations, you are live on the new system, but your job is not done. There are a host of things to do to continue to get maximum value from your system.

In addition to the chronology of events listed above, we are also going to talk about software development and software testing to give the reader some insight into how the software development cycle works within a vendor.

📖 Talk the Talk: A Glossary of Select Business Terms

In 2007, IBM[4] aired a commercial that was based on the fictitious gameshow called 'Buzzword Bingo' (see on YouTube). It was damn funny because it was such a quality mocking of the language that is used in the software business. I have kept a list of favorite buzzwords and terms that I have encountered over the years. I'm not suggesting that you should actually use most of these terms, but you gotta be able to talk the talk!

GUI (pronounced gooey)

The first day I am working at a software company, I am invited to a status meeting. They were making fun of the fact that the new guy (me) was wearing a tie but once they tired of that, they were all talking about the GUI. I had no idea what they were talking about. Many years later I casually use the term like everyone on the planet knows what it means. It turns out that the GUI is the graphical user interface of a software application, so essentially the screens (or web pages/forms) that the user interacts with to actually use the software. In recent years, the 'G' seems to have been dropped (I guess we just assume it is now graphical) and call it a UI (pronounced you-eye not you-ee).

SME (pronounced smee)

A SME is a Subject Matter Expert, meaning he/she knows a lot about something. I'm not sure who invented this term - I checked the web and couldn't come up with anything reliable. I wish I could unhear this term but I think it is with me for good so I pass it along to pollute your mind as well.

Best of Breed

I first heard 'Best of Breed' many years ago when I had just started working in my first real software job. I have heard it used in many ways since and in several industries. To do something 'Best of Breed' means you are going to pick components that are the best at what they handle and then combine them to get a superior solution. The alternative is a one-stop shopping approach where all needs were met with a single application but that solution may not be as powerful as the combined capabilities of the Best of Breed approach. Best of Breed is a fine strategy, but the term has become overused in the marketing of software and has become pretty much a cliché.

Gap (Gap Analysis)

Remember the Gap Band[5] from the 80's? – 'You dropped a bomb on me – baby ... ' Great song – I'm listening to it right now on Napster.

If you are evaluating a software system for your business it is likely that the software does not provide a feature or capability that your business needs to function. This shortcoming is referred to as a gap. To analyze a system for these shortcomings is called a Gap Analysis. Gaps can be dealt with by changing the software, using an alternative workflow, or determining the requirement is obsolete.

Scope Creep (Creep)

No – it's not a person looking at you with a telescope. When a project is established, it generally has definition or boundaries to the functionality and capabilities that will be available. This is referred to as scope. To use the word scope, you might say 'we need to limit the scope of the project only to the most important features to keep costs low'. But what happens when Sally, the project sponsor, starts asking for additional features or niceties? We call that scope creep – the scope is increasing and making the project bigger. More on scope creep in later parts of the book.

Socialize

To socialize is to share something with your peers. 'Thanks for sending along the brochure on your products. Let me socialize with my team and get back to you with feedback.' I just call it 'sharing' but that doesn't sound as hip or cool as socialize.

Lift

To get 'Lift' is to get value or some efficiency from a project. I have heard it more on the west coast from non-technical folks but it has made its way east as well. Let me use in a sentence: 'Getting this phase of the project live will give us some much-needed lift'. What is the origin of this term? I'm thinking either a.) aeronautical analogy to getting wind under your wings to pick up an airplane, or b.) inspired by a Victoria's Secret commercial.

Current State / Future State

Doesn't exactly roll off the tongue but essentially translates to 'the crappy way we do something now versus the awesome way we are going to do it in the future when we have cool new software'. A beaver using in a non-software sentence: 'In its current state, this stream flows freely and makes it hard for me to catch food but in the future state, my new dam will allow me to catch fish at my leisure.'

Swag

Swag has two different meanings:

1.) A Sophisticated Wild Ass Guess – an initial software estimate that may use any number of estimation methods but at the end of the day is just a guess on how long it is going to take to do something. I have heard the word 'sophisticated' replaced with other less professional words.

2.) Stuff that you get such as hats, t-shirts, pens, etc. at trade shows or when a vendor comes to visit you. Client using in a sentence: 'Looking forward to seeing you next week – make sure to bring my troops some good swag.'

Chapter 2: The Search - Selecting a Software Product

Your firm wants to buy a new accounting system. Seems fairly straightforward – let's think about what features we want, talk to a bunch of vendors, and pick the one that fits the best. Our development team thinks we should just build our own –they say it would save us money and we would get exactly what we want. There are many ways to perform a software search and different firms have policies and processes that they need to follow. My goal in this section is to talk about the important elements of a search and some of the pitfalls or opportunities you may encounter during the search process.

Can't We Just Outsource the Whole Thing?

I'm going to talk briefly about outsourcing here and then dive into it deeper in a later chapter. I bring it up here because it is normally a key topic that comes up when a firm is deciding on the best software-related decision for their business. There are several levels of outsourcing that I have seen:

- **Full Lift-out** – the business function is no longer done by your firm – it is completely outsourced to another firm. The key with this is that not only the software component is gone but also the operational function and staffing associated with it.

- **Hosted** – the vendor is responsible for providing the software and the hardware infrastructure, however your firm keeps operational control over using the software.

- **Insource** – less common but the vendor is responsible for running the software and associated operational aspects but it is run on hardware inside the firm.

There are benefits, drawbacks, and costs associated with outsourcing and I think firms make a mistake in thinking that outsourcing is a shortcut to the overall evaluation process. Let's do a full evaluation of what is best for our firm and <u>then</u> decide if some level of outsourcing is a good choice.

Buy vs. Build

To 'buy' is to purchase a commercial software product. To 'build' is to have programmers write software specifically for you.

Arguments for Buy:

- Safety in numbers – if other firms are using the software as you intend to use it then good bet that it works.

- The software likely has features that you wouldn't build but you will ultimately find useful to your business.

- Shared investment across the client base means that it should be cheaper than incurring the full cost of development.

- Faster implementation cycle because the software already exists – we don't have to build it first before implementing it.

Arguments for Build:

- We get exactly what we want.

- We control the development schedule and can enhance as necessary in the future.

- We are unique – nobody does what we do.

If you are considering a build, there are some practical considerations that your development team likely won't tell you that should be considered carefully:

- Developers want to build – they have a bias – it is simply more fun for them to build their own stuff than to implement someone else's application. They generally do not look at the project as a way to make the firm more efficient - they look at it as an opportunity to work in new technologies and learn new stuff.

- Developers underestimate development costs. The reason is that they think only about the effort to write the code – they do not consider the costs of testing, workflow analysis, and the future coding that will be required to keep the application running on future operating systems or browsers.

- Building will be time consuming for your business users. Building software requires a lot of analysis and testing – things your developers should not and do not want to be doing.

- Does your development team have the skills to build a commercial grade application? Are you qualified to assess this?

- What happens if the developer(s) who built the application moves on to another job (they will)? Do you have the source code and expertise to maintain the application without them?

- What is your support model? Are the developers going to commit to being on call on weekends, etc.?

The practical guidance on 'Build' is that unless you fall into one of the below buckets, be very cautious about choosing to build software that you can otherwise buy:

- You have an experienced development team that has a track record of building complex software.

- You have a truly unique software problem that you cannot buy commercially.

- The software is 'secret sauce' for the firm that gives you competitive advantage and it is not something you want to share with competitors.

Best of Both Worlds - Buy AND Build?

Sometimes the right answer might be somewhere in the middle.

Often in a software search, the evaluators are looking to see if the software can do everything that the firm wants/needs it to be able to do. Many firms have unique workflows or 'isms' (think weird-isms, or unique-isms) that are going to make it very hard to find a software package that handles specifically what they want to be able to do. In this case, maybe the best solution is to pick the system that does the standard stuff most effectively AND has the **extensibility** that would allow your development team to integrate some custom software into the platform. We will talk about extensibility more later, but it is a big consideration that is often forgotten when evaluating software. A product that is extensible allows your firm flexibility to interact with the software in different ways:

- Data extraction

- Custom screens/navigations

- Access to business logic (APIs/programmatic interfaces)

I'm just planting the seed that there is a middle ground between buy and build and for evaluators to keep an open mind during the evaluation process.

No Buy / No Build

Don't forget that one of the options available is to you is not a software option at all. Through your analysis and due diligence, you may find that there is not an appreciably better system out there or that it is operational changes that are necessary more so than software changes. This sometimes gets lost in the enthusiasm of the process but should not be overlooked as an option.

🤝 Spreadsheets Are Like Krispy Kreme Donuts

Have you ever had a Krispy Kreme Donut[†] – good, right? Take that same donut and put in in a microwave for 10 seconds – it is crazy good, exponentially better! Take your second donut – 10 seconds – more wow. I can do one more. 10 seconds. Ok – I went too far. I'm starting to shake from the sugar. Hour later – why do I have this terrible headache? Spreadsheets are like Krispy Kreme Donuts – let me explain. We once did an experiment like this when I was in a college economics class to demonstrate the concept of 'diminishing marginal utility'. I challenge you to use this term in a meaningful way in a business meeting. Diminishing marginal utility means that you get less value/satisfaction as you continue to do the same thing.

Spreadsheets are awesome. They are the Swiss Army knife of technology. Excel (us 80's kids learned on Lotus 1-2-3[6]) has fundamentally done the same thing for the last 20 years but evolution in conditional formatting, data integration, and years of additional functional goodies have made it even more versatile. I have built some bad ass spreadsheets in my day and still love building stuff in them.

Excel is a terrific tool for modeling, data movement, and file parsing. However, it is NOT a great application development tool, but much like the donut addict - users cannot stop themselves.

Here is an example of how it usually goes:

_____

[†] Krispy Kreme makes different flavors of donuts but I am talking about the original glaze version only. If you microwave longer than 10 seconds do at your own risk – they get molten hot and nothing kills the experiment more than a 3rd degree burn to the roof of your mouth.

We are a startup and need to do some reporting to our clients. We only have a few clients, so can someone build a spreadsheet that will allow us to type in some information and have it output with graphs and stuff so it looks nice? No problem. Life goes on and we sign some more clients and on month-ends, Judy is working over the weekend to get all the spreadsheets done. We hire another operations person to help Judy – all good for six months. But we sign more clients and now both Judy and Bob are working month-ends to get the increasingly large number of spreadsheets done. Bob says 'this sucks' and quits. Judy tells her boss that they should hire two people to replace Bob, otherwise they are susceptible to the same problem going forward but it will be worse because by then there will be even more work to do. You get the idea.

This is a classic Excel issue. Users don't know when they need to abandon Excel as their solution – it worked so good to start but it slowly transforms into a risk. The basis of this problem is that Excel generally doesn't scale. We will talk about scalability at other times in the book but the above example is one of a lack of operational scale. We have built and implemented a lot of software over the years to replace Excel 'applications'. Unfortunately, Excel applications are normally not replaced until management is freaking out due to the amount of hiring that must be done to keep things running smoothly. This is when they consider that maybe they need real software to deal with the problem.

The Spreadsheet High:

- So easy, so powerful

- Great learning stepping stone (ranges, functions, macros, oh my!)

- Shareable – everyone has it

- Cheap

The Hangover:

- Not scalable from volume or operational standpoint

- Not multi-user

- Not 'real' database

- Complex spreadsheets are prone to high risk mistakes

Excel is one of my favorite software things EVER but it is <u>not</u> a great tool for building software. Love it and use it but know the signs of when it should be replaced by something more durable.

Let the Search Begin!

For the remainder of this chapter, we are going to assume that there is some 'Buy' component to your decision and therefore you need to go select some software. At a high level, the search process can take many paths but the most conventional is as follows:

- Create a long list – Do some research, introductory demos. We once won a deal where we were told there were 27 products in the initial long list – that is a record for me. Less than eight is more the norm.

- Create short list – Maybe three vendors, RFIs, longer demos.

- Target vendor – Pricing, negotiations, final due diligence, references, contract.

Buyers are from Mars, Vendors are from Pluto[‡]

In 1992, John Gray, PhD wrote the bestselling relationship book *Men are from Mars, Women are from Venus*[7]. The overview in Amazon describes it as a 'classic guide to understanding the opposite sex'. It also says that he has sold over 50 million books – I bet I won't sell even half that many but you never know! The gist of the book is that men and women are wired differently and understanding those differences can help a guy better understand how not to annoy his wife (that is my interpretation anyway).

_____

[‡] When I was a boy, Pluto was a planet. I know some now say it is not, but using it in my metaphor is my way of protesting – It will always be a planet to me.

I started thinking about software buyers and vendors and that the two parties are also wired and motivated quite differently.

Vendors:

- Software salespeople want to do a software deal – that is their job. They are going to do everything they can to make their software seem like a good fit (even if it is not). Remember that software salespeople are not judged on how successful software is for the buyer – they are judged (and compensated) on whether they do the deal. This seems obvious but don't forget.

- Software firms generally think about the world in terms of how their software works. They will use their terminology and generally assume that you think of the problem they solve in the same way that they do.

- Software firms assume you know what they know and generally like to talk about technology.

Buyers:

- Buyers care less about the actual software and more about their workflows and how a vendor's system will help them achieve their business needs.

- Buyers do not like re-engineering their workflows. They will often claim that they do but generally they do not.

- There are some firms that are particularly well versed at buying and evaluating software but most firms are not. This creates situations where buyers are not sure what they actually bought and sets up a real opportunity for buyer remorse.

Buyers - Do We Know What We Are Looking to Buy?

It sounds a little simple but as a buyer, do you know what you are looking to buy? My experience is that some buyers are very prepared to go into the evaluation process but other buyers are pretty naïve about what they are looking for and how to pick an appropriate solution. The well-prepared buyers have done some or all of the following steps:

RFI/RFP

A 'Request for Information' or a 'Request for Proposal' is generally a formal document that a buyer will send to a software vendor to learn more about the software, services, and operating aspects of the company. As a vendor, we got a lot of RFIs from firms doing a software search. On the one hand, it is time consuming and often painful to do a thorough job completing an RFI, but on the other hand, it was an indicator to us that a.) the firm was serious about their search, and b.) the questions gave us some insight into their workflow and needs that would allow us to better prepare for their demo.

The terms RFI and RFP are often used interchangeably, however the RFI is generally viewed as an information request only while the RFP typically refers to a vendor providing a bid or a pricing proposal.

I like the RFI/RFP concept, but like all things, it can go off the rails in the wrong hands so here is my shortlist to preparing a good one:

- Do the workflow and overall needs analysis up front and understand the core needs and capabilities that you are looking for. Use these as the basis of your questions.

- Vendors will do a better job answering your request if you keep it concise. The 100-page monster boilerplate RFP that comes out of the corporate procurement department is the one that the vendors dread. Another approach is to do a mini-RFI to get a list of vendors together and then give the final RFP to just the shortlist vendors.

- Give the vendors a reasonable deadline – at least a few weeks to turn around.

- Ask for List Pricing – It is important to get a sense of a.) how a vendor prices (users, servers, volumes, etc.), and b.) what is the anticipated cost in relation to the other vendors? I want to know if my potential vendors are in relatively the same ballpark or if there is a significant dispersion in pricing.   I have never liked the concept of asking a vendor for their 'best' price at this point in the process – there is time for negotiating later.

- Disclose that the vendor's request responses will be included as part of the final licensing agreement – not everyone does this but it's smart. Some software sales folks can get a bit optimistic/creative when describing the capabilities of their system and this inclusion provides some accountability for the answers provided by the vendor.

Research Firms and Third-Party Search Consultants

Buyers will often engage a research firm or a third-party consultant to assist with the software search process. This can often make a lot of sense for the following reasons:

- They have knowledge of the vendors in the industry and familiarity with the specific products.

- They have other clients who are using these products.

- They are often good at drafting an RFI and helping the buyer with workflow and needs analysis.

All good things. However, understand who you are working with and the motivations and potential conflicts of interest that can exist for these firms:

- Research – Research firms sell their research to buyers – that is their business. Before taking that research as gospel, consider:

  - How old is the research? – Things change quickly in the software world. Are there new or uncovered vendors to consider?

  - How thorough is the research? – As a vendor, we were covered by some great research firms who really took the time to learn about our offering. We were also covered by others who would do a review based on a very superficial understanding of our products.

  - Do vendors have to pay to be 'covered' by the research firm? Payment is not always in hard dollars. Understand conflict of interest situations – they are real and not uncommon.

- Search Vendors

  - It is easy to claim to be in the vendor search business – you just have to say that you do them. But that doesn't mean that you are good at it. Run references – find out if a firm has specific expertise in your specific domain and if they have a solid track record with other firms.

  - Does the search vendor have any direct or indirect relationship with vendors in the search universe? We worked with a client several years back who found out that the consultant that assisted them with a software search received 70% of its revenues providing implementation services on the system that they recommended. The buyer was understandably upset that they did not receive objective assistance from the consultant. Request a disclosure from the search vendor on any direct or indirect relationships with the software vendors.

Caveat Emptor – Buyer Beware

Getting help with your search can be great but make sure there is no conflict of interest for those assisting you. The best way to find out is to a.) have the consultant attest to their position in your written agreement, and b.) run references - preferably ones that you can obtain on your own.

🚚 The Power of Omission (What You Say/What You Mean)

One of my work pals used to often say that a joke is 90% truth. Here are a few that might fit in that category:

Vendor Says:	Vendor Means:
We can do that	With enough time and money, we can do just about anything
That's in the next release	That is possibly a good idea and could find itself in some release someday
We'd like to partner with you	We'd like you to give us money to build something that we both want
It is fully regression tested	Run your own tests and let us know if everything works
Let us get back to you on that	We don't want to talk about this anymore and need to move on with demo – I am pretending to write it down for later follow up

Two more:

Salesperson tells the prospective client that the cost will be $100k/year.

Buyer: Ok

Salesperson thinks: This is awesome – they have no issues with my pricing – this one is in the bag!

Buyer really means: 'I have heard that you just said $100k and I am saying Ok to confirm that I heard you – we will negotiate at a later time.'

**Agreeing on a deadline.**

Developer to Product Manager: I can get that coded in a week.

Developer really means: It will take me a day to code that but I'm going to get interrupted by other people throughout the week and have other stuff on my plate so my estimate is a week.

Product Manager: It's not going to take a week – you are padding! How about 3 days?

Ace a Technology Job Interview

I have interviewed lots of candidates for many types of positions and continue to be amazed by how many people bring me the same unappealing lines. I don't consider myself a particularly good interviewer and generally don't have a standard methodology or list of questions for interrogating people. I can remember making only one candidate cry. I have cut interviews short if I think the candidate misrepresented themselves. Overall, I want to figure out a.) if I would like to work with you on a day to day basis, b.) do you bring real skills to the party, and c.) your level of enthusiasm. There are plenty of great books written on interviewing and job search but I've boiled down a short list of my key bullets.

Avoid this:

- I'm a generalist – jack of all trades master of none – I have heard this a shocking number of times – I want you to be a master of something!

- What 'We' did – I honestly stop about 50% of the interviews I do and explain to the candidate that I don't care what their team is good at – I care what you, the individual, are good at. I'm not interviewing your team – I am interviewing you. After explaining this, about 50% of candidates continue to talk about what their team does. I just assume you have no individual skills and try and wrap up the interview.

- I'm a problem solver looking for a problem – barf me out – gag me with a spoon![8] (Moon Unit Zappa - Valley Girls). I can't believe I have heard this, much less, multiple times.

- Fast learner – yeah, ok – tell me what you know and what you learned fast but more importantly, how **well** do you know what you learned. Fast is less important to me than mastery – tell me about your mastery.

- I can read code but not write it. Well, that is fascinating! – I have positions open for people who can write good code but no positions for 'code readers'. I know you are trying to make yourself sound more technically proficient but you can do better than that!

- I've been meaning to brush up on my technical skills – Again, I think that is great but I notice in your resume that you have not been working for the last eight months. Do you think you could have squeezed in a little learning time so instead you could say 'I did some online classes to learn html, CSS, and a little JavaScript'? Nice job – shows some initiative!

- Alphabet soup – a lot of resumes (particularly technical ones) like to list every technology they have ever heard of: C, C++, C#, JavaScript, Perl, Python, Oracle, Paradox, VisiCalc, ... I think that is fine within reason but a.) I would leave the dated technology off unless you are specifically looking for job in that area. I'm sure you are proud of the Fortran coding you did 30 years ago, but listing it is not really going to do anything except make you look dated. And b.) if it is on the list, be prepared to talk about it as it is fair game for me to dig into it. When I hear 'I don't know much about it but my team used it' - see above.

- How do you think the company would fit my lifestyle? I'm sorry – you are at an interview to sell me on the fact that you would be great for the role. You are not picking a summer camp. This is typically a younger candidate entitlement mentality. Ask these questions in a 2nd or 3rd interview in a less obnoxious way – sell me on your value as an employee first.

- Greatest weakness question – lots of interviewers like this question. Do not answer: 'My greatest weakness is that I don't think I have any weaknesses.' The first guy who said it probably got a laugh but the next million are just unimaginative and annoying.

- Final things I should not even have to say but have had enough interviews that violate so I will list:

  o Wear something nice/appropriate to an interview – yeah, it still matters, even in today's casual dress society. I may never need to see it again but nice to know you can don a suit if necessary.

  o Do not smell like cigarettes, overpowering cologne/perfume, or any other worse olfactory violations.

  o Be on time – it amazes me how many people are late for interviews. Leave an hour earlier and have a cup of coffee if you arrive early.

  o Bring a hard copy of your resume.

Top Good:

- **Speak in Specifics** – tell me about how you impacted a project and the things that you did on the project to make it successful. Use specific examples or cases that show off your hands-on skills and domain knowledge.

- **What Are Your Skills?** – what are you are good at and what do you bring to the party that will make our business better? Things like 'hard worker' and 'plays well with others' aren't really skills.

- **Self-Deprecation** – there is a fine line between cocky and confident and most interviewers like confident but not over confident. A great way to keep on the good side is to make fun of yourself a little bit. It shows you have a sense of humor and don't take yourself too seriously.

- **Work Ethic** – give me examples of hard work and taking initiative. Old fashioned work ethic will never go out of style.

Vendor Demos

You have your RFIs back, have talked to the vendors and are ready to do some demos. Very exciting!

Whether you are doing an introductory demo or a deeper dive follow-up session, it is important to get on the same page as to how you want to spend the time effectively. Working this out ahead of time makes it better for both buyer and vendor because you are not working out preferences on the fly.

Demo Prep and Manners

There are a few guidelines that I think help to make a demo successful.

- We did a lot of intro demos via WebEx[9] or other remote meeting software. It is a great way to do a cost-effective intro demo. If it is convenient to do in person, then great, but as a vendor I always felt that flying across the country to do an intro demo was a bit of overkill. For a second or deeper dive session, I absolutely wanted to be onsite.

- If the meeting is onsite, get connectivity and equipment worked out up front. We used to require our sales staff to have a local version of a demo that could be run on a laptop as well as bring a portable projector to all demos. We later required that all demos needed a portable wireless internet as well, in the event that we could not use the client's internet connection. Even if the prospective client claimed that they have all the necessary equipment, here is what goes wrong (a lot):

  - They have a projector but it is an 80's vintage machine that runs VGA resolution so I can only get 25% of my application on the screen. Essentially impossible to do a good demo on this screen.

- They have a widescreen TV/monitor but only a 50-inch screen in a room that holds 30 people. Only the first few people can actually see it. I can make my portable projector about 3 times bigger.

- At the last minute, the prospect says 'Bob is not in office today so we will need to do a WebEx'. Cannot get on the internet because we were not pre-cleared by corporate security to get a security key to get on the network or nobody knows the guest password.

- The prospect has $50k of state of the art audio/video equipment in the room, but:

  - They don't know how to use it because it is so complicated.

  - An external laptop cannot be plugged into it.

  - There are no power plugs within 30 feet of the conference table and no power strips or extension cords are available.

You get the idea. All these things have happened at least once and others, dozens of times. We just planned that we had to bring our own stuff and I'd estimate that at about one third of all demos we would not use the prospect's equipment. This doesn't seem like a big thing but it really is important and can make or break a demo – I put it at the top of the prep list for vendor and prospect to get worked out.

- Late attendee – Don't show up to demo late and then start asking questions. Particularly annoying if you preface your question with 'You may have already covered this but …'. Yeah – we did cover it and you are making me waste time covering it again. Come as late as you want but don't make me start over for you.

- Impatient attendee – Don't be the 'just show me the product' guy. The vendor may want to open with a few slides to talk about the company, product positioning, and an overview of what will be covered in the demo. I get it that you don't want to see 50 PowerPoint slides but give me the opportunity as a vendor to set the table. In an intro demo, I generally wanted my intro to be 5-8 minutes with less than 10 slides.

- Hijacker attendee – Don't be the meeting hijacker. I'm all for fielding questions, but when the same person is on his 8th question in the first fifteen minutes of the meeting and taking the conversation down obscure paths, it would be good for a leader at the prospect to throw the vendor a bone and ask that questions be held until we get through the core agenda.

- Vendor – Stick to your allotted time. Don't go begging for another 30 minutes at the end of the meeting. It is your responsibility to keep the meeting moving and get your best message across in the agreed upon meeting time. Avoid giving five minute, tangent laden answers to questions and you should be good.

- Meeting recording – As a vendor, I did not like our demos being recorded. The main reason is that I did not want the possibility that the recording would get in the hands of our competitors. I have been asked in meetings if the WebEx could be recorded and our general answer was 'No' but we made a few exceptions. The request was normally based on the position that certain people could not make the demo and that they could watch the recording at a later time. We were always willing to schedule follow-up demos and thought it was far more effective to be able to interact with these people instead of them watching a recording (which I'm pretty certain they would rarely do). We did find out once (and I'm sure there were more) that the prospect recorded on their WebEx without telling us – not cool – a breach of ethics to me.

Introductory Demo

An introductory demo is a buyer's first chance to see a vendor's software and get an overall sense of its capabilities. An intro demo for me was optimally 90 minutes, although 60 minutes was not unusual and I would get the 'show me what you have in 30 minutes'.   The reason I like 90 minutes is that I could follow a reasonable format that allowed for questions and didn't make me want to speak twice as fast as I normally would. Something like below is a standard 90-minute layout. You can do in an hour but what seems to happen is that it becomes a quick vendor overview and then the demo and then we all say 'thanks' and we hang up. Having a little post-demo time is good for both parties.

- Introductions/Tell me a little about your business – 10 minutes

- Vendor Overview – 10 minutes

- Core Demo – 50 minutes

- Questions – 15 minutes

- Wrap-up/Next Steps – 5 minutes

We talked earlier about the prep for a demo but a few notes on an initial demo:

- Let the vendor do their demo. Let them follow their script. I know you have questions but try and keep to a minimum. You want to learn about all the capabilities of the system so sit back and listen. They may have capabilities you never thought of but if you don't let them get there, you will never see it. This demo should be designed to show you all their best stuff. There will be time in the future for digging into your needs. A demo should have a flow to it. Most of the stuff that people ask to see, I respond 'we will be getting to that in a few minutes' so I can keep on my script. Just be a little patient.

- Start on time. If you are giving me 60 minutes, please don't waste 10 minutes waiting for everyone to show up – start the meeting. As stated earlier, we were never hesitant to do follow up introductory demos to a firm. We saw it as a good indicator of interest and an opportunity to get to know them better. What sucks is getting 30 minutes – that forces you to rush and do a crappy job that doesn't represent the offering properly.

- See prep and manners in earlier section.

🚐 Vendors: Top Things for a Great Software Demo

1. **Agreed upon agenda.** Total Time, Allocation of Time, Attendees – I want to know how long I have and who I am talking to – is it a business and/or technical audience, are their senior management folks in room? These variables will allow me to tailor my message most appropriately. A good salesperson will use this prep time to get a plan together and build a working relationship with the prospective client.

2. **Do a concise introduction and wrap-up.** (no exhausting PowerPoint deck) – Set the table about the case you are going to make, make your case and then re-emphasize your key points. Some people ask to just dive into a demo but senior managers want to know a bit about your company and overall positioning.

   "Tell the audience what you're going to say, say it; then tell them what you've said." Dale Carnegie[10]

3. **Get feedback from prospect** on what makes them unique and key success factors for them <u>before the demo</u> and then use that information in your demo. This helps you decide if you should emphasize certain features, understand client's current process and workflow, and how you can best present your solution. Most clients will take a call to discuss if you ask.

   'Help me help you'

   Jerry to Rod Tidwell from movie Jerry McGuire[11]

4. **Quality data in your demo.** I have seen a lot of bad data in demos. The data in your demo should tell a story and be information that the buyer can identify with. Examples:

   - If I am working with a collection of sample accounts, give them real names (not test1, test2, ...)

- If I am a selling to a healthcare company, show me healthcare data not financial services data.

You may want to convince yourself that this doesn't really matter but it does. I have heard a lot of feedback from buyers looking at potential software and this comes up frequently.

- Show me data that is dated currently – If I am doing a demo but the dates I am using are eight years old, people may not say anything about it but they are thinking negative thoughts about it. Having good data in your demo can be time consuming to maintain and update but it is critical because:

  o Crappy data makes you, as a vendor, look lazy.

  o Users cannot identify with what you are trying to say. They are trying to relate their problems to your data that is not reflective of their business and therefore, you lose them. Great data does just the opposite – it reinforces that you understand their business and makes it easy for them to relate your product to their business.

5. **Script your demo**. A software demo should be scripted to organize and present your solution in a thoughtful and straightforward way. The script should consist of mini-demo modules that are a combination of a.) point/feature I want to make, and b.) the clicks and data that I will show to make this point. Scripting your demo has a few key benefits:

- Creating the script helps you organize your thoughts and the demo structure. We created scripts that we thought were good but once we tried them out, decided it really wasn't great so we would change them. Remember that you have about an hour to show someone something that they have never seen before.

- Consistency – I want all the people in my company delivering essentially the same demo. I know that people have different 'styles' but it was important that whoever was presenting put forth the key features in a way that we had decided was most effective. I am all for modifying your demo to fit the audience, but you, as a demo person, need to demonstrate that you can deliver the standard demo well before you are certified to do them.

6. **Anecdotal demo.** Make your demo an interesting story not an exercise in showing screens. Think about the business users who are watching your demo – they are trying to figure out how your offering fits their business. Don't just show them screenshots. Tell them a story or example of how another client handles a situation and support that story with what you are showing on the screen. We always used the term 'anecdotal demo', meaning – talk about how different firms handle situations and creative solutions. Clients love to hear about what others are doing and how they are doing it.

7. **Maximize stick-forward moments.** During presidential debates, the networks have a real-time technology that they use on focus groups to determine how positive or negative a candidate's message is. Each person in the focus group gets a joystick controller that allows the user to push the stick forward on positive comments, back on negative, and leave in the middle when neutral. The network then takes this feedback and charts it in the aggregate to show if what the person is saying is popular or not. Although we do not have this technology for our demos, we used the analogy to say that we wanted as many 'stick forward' moments in the demo as possible. People respond very well to seeing something that applies to their business problem and addresses a challenge or situation that is currently painful for them. Your job is to unearth as many of these as possible and if you do, good things will happen.

8. **Anticipate questions**. Know the questions people are going to ask and have examples ready to answer them. When you ask me a question in a demo, I can either a.) answer your question, or b.) show you how the software solves your question. Show is the more powerful answer but it takes work to have things setup and ready to go in anticipation of questions. I used to write down the key questions we got after a demo and made a point to add examples to our demo environment that made it easy for us to demonstrate our solutions to those questions. It takes time and effort, but over time you build up a nice set of supporting examples that help your overall demo.

9. **Have 'A' team people presenting demos**. If you have one opportunity to make a first impression, then make sure the person doing your demo is good at it. Many firms have sales engineers or product managers do demos as they understand the business and the software better than the sales people and can quickly have an interactive conversation with the prospect. I have met some sales people who are good at demoing software but many are not (even though they think they are). Salespeople have an important role but performing demos is not necessarily the best fit for them. Who handles the demo can have a dramatic impact. I have seen the same product demoed by two different people with vastly different expertise in the product and it is amazing how different the demo can be. The experienced demo gets you to the next round – the inexperienced demo likely gets you eliminated.

10. **Be respectful of timeframes and keep yourself on schedule**. It is your job as the presenter to keep things on track. Don't get sidetracked for 15 minutes on one question. You may get some additional time at the end but don't assume you will. 'I just need 10 more minutes to show you some other stuff' is begging and unseemly.

11. **Follow up on the things you say you will follow up on**. Often overlooked are questions in a demo that the presenter does not know the answer to – that is ok. We have all said many times in a

demo 'let us get back to you on that' but rarely does anyone get back. It is the sales person's job to write these things down and get back to the prospect with answers to these issues. It provides the vendor a natural follow-up and demonstrates that they follow through on things.

Making Your Short List

Vendors have filled out your RFI and have provided your team an initial demo. It is time to create a short list of vendors who you will dig into deeper.

Demo Score Cards

Prospective clients sometimes like to make scorecards that people involved in the search process can use to score a vendor. There are normally multiple sections that identify functional features or preferences that the client is looking for with a weighting to set the emphasis of the functional feature. I have mixed feelings on the scorecard concept:

Positives:

- Forces the prospective client to think about what is important to them – this analysis is important and shows that the buyer has some clarity on their goals.

- Provides a consistent set of criteria for the evaluators.

Negatives:

- The scorecard is often laden with soft or subjective things that are hard to quantify and may have no impact on your overall success. 'Application looks modern' is an evaluation criteria I once saw for a non-client facing application. Is this a critical evaluation element?

- Who is filling out the card? – If one person gives a vendor a score of 1 and another person scores it a 5, does this mean that the person who gave a score of 1 just doesn't understand?

- Individuals in the process can have preferences toward vendors and can low score the other vendors to give their favorite an advantage.

If you are going to utilize the scorecard, a few recommendations:

1.) Use the scores as a component to your decision-making process but not the only determinant. What if a vendor has great functionality but their technology is a complete 'no' for you? Pick your short list using all available information. I once worked with a client who said that their process was to add up all the scores on vendors and the top three weighted scored vendors were the short list vendors – period. They said it was the only fair and objective way to do it. You don't have to justify being fair – your job is to pick the best vendors for your needs using whatever information you think applicable.

2.) Everyone's score does not need to count equally. Look for situations where there is variation on score across evaluators and get to the bottom of why there is a discrepancy – it is typically a lack of understanding that you can talk through or work with the vendor to clarify.

3.) Most importantly, share the score card with the vendors. Plenty of prospects told us we couldn't see the evaluation criteria – this seems ridiculous to me. Don't you want me to know what I am being graded on? You don't have to show me the scores but sharing the criteria just helps me do a better demo – sometimes I feel like I am in kindergarten.

Deep Dive Due Diligence

You have gotten down to a short list of vendors and really want to dig into the software to figure out the best fit. Once you have reached this point, it is time to step up your due diligence with the goal of identifying the top vendor. There are many ways to work through this process. I am going to focus on the key things that I recommend evaluating at this point in the process:

Expanded Demo/Working Session

When you reach the finalist round as a vendor, the prospective client will likely want to do an extended demo / working session to further evaluate your offering. Some firms will want to essentially present a longer version of the first demo, but the more prepared firms will generally prepare use cases and examples of what they want to see and turn the session into a Proof of Concept session. The preparation for this can be very time consuming for the vendors depending on the demands of the prospect, but I think it is important for the prospective client to evaluate products specific to their business instead of just generally. When putting together use cases, a few general guidelines:

- Clients like to see their own data in the vendor's system and used in the use case process. This is generally a good idea but provide the data to the vendor in a complete and easy to import format. I'd say more than half of the data that clients asked us to use was incomplete or not machine readable.

- Use cases can vary significantly depending on the type of system that you are evaluating. Use cases for an accounting system may be more focused on proof that the system can handle the necessary calculations while the use cases for a Customer Relationship Management system (CRM) might be much more workflow focused. The important thing here is to determine how you want to evaluate: a.) can the system handle my requirement?, and b.) do we like how the system can accomplish it?

📖 Glossary of Development/Infrastructure Terms

The next section talks about reviewing software from a technical standpoint so below are a few terms that might be helpful.

Engine / Business Layer

This is essentially all the software that is not the GUI (see earlier definition). I know – all the engineers will tell me about the business layer, tiers, and other stuff and that I am oversimplifying.

Refactor

This was a favorite in my office and I got so sick of hearing it that I had to outlaw its use for a while. To 'refactor' code is to change how it is structurally built such that it can be used or accessed differently than it was originally intended. There are many times when a good refactoring is necessary and productive. My issue with the term is the rewriting of poorly written code is also often called 'refactor'. Just say it like it is – if it was done poorly in the first place, just say so. The problem with refactoring (from a business standpoint) is that it normally requires a bunch of testing and doesn't necessarily give me anything new. A necessary evil but it costs me money and I don't get anything tangible – this makes me grumpy.

Server

Early in my career when I heard of people talking about servers I assumed it was a special kind of hardware. It is true that a server can be a specialized kind of hardware but that is not what makes it a server. It is the function that the machine serves that makes it a server. Your laptop can be a server if you are hosting a website on it. As the name implies, a server is designed to provide a service to another computer.

Client

A client is a device that gets something from a server. Think of it as the opposite of a server – A client is a consumer of something. A simple example in a web application is a browser getting web pages from a web server. You may also hear the terms 'thick' or 'thin' client. The thickness of a client refers to the amount of business logic that is built into the client software. A thin client has very little logic while a thick client has a lot.

Middle Tier/Service Layer

Many current software applications have multiple processing layers to help with scalability, security, and other processing benefits. When you hear the terms middle tiers, service layers, etc., they are referring to these components of a software application. Not really clear? It's ok, sort of a techie thing.

P to V (Physical to Virtual)

A Canadian associate of mine used to love to say 'P to V' – it just rolls off the tongue. To P to V a server means to turn it from a physical server to a virtual server. Virtual servers (Virtual Machines or VMs) have become big over the last several years as it is easy to maintain many virtual machines on a single physical server. Virtualization allows multiple 'computers' to run on a single physical computer. A simple example would be running both Windows and Mac operating systems on your laptop. Another cool benefit of VMs is that they are essentially files so it makes it easy to move or copy a version of a computer to a different place. If you have a physical server, you can convert it to a virtual server – this is the process of P to V'ing.

Bounce the Server (Cycle)

Has anyone ever told you to reboot or restart your computer? It's that but with a cooler name. Does rebooting really ever work? Actually – yes, and the general reason is that processes and memory are released by the process so you sort of start fresh. The origin of the term is that the server goes down and then comes up (like a bouncing ball).

SDLC (Software Development Life Cycle)

SDLC refers to the methodology a firm uses to create software. 'So, tell me about your SDLC'. 'Well, our Software Development Life Cycle could best be described as a modified waterfall methodology with a good dose of scrum mixed in.'   There are lots of methodologies or processes that firms use to build software. Terms like Waterfall, Scrum, RAD are cool names assigned to describe these methods. For example, a Waterfall approach is a more traditional linear approach to development where Scrum or RAD are more iterative and based on prototyping. One methodology requires me to stand up in meetings instead of using a chair – I generally prefer a chair but that isn't hip and trendy. Think of them as diet plans: South Beach, Weight Watchers – they all are trying to get you to drop pounds – just describing a varying approach to diet and exercise.

Scalable

We will talk about scalability at other times in the book but when a non-technical person asks if software is scalable they are generally asking of it can handle large volumes of data/output in a reasonable timeframe. If a technical person is asking, they are trying to learn how the software can be utilized on a larger or distributed hardware infrastructure to allow the product to handle increasing demand. Technical folks will bristle at this oversimplified description but for our purposes, I think it's ok.

Technical Review

A technical review of a vendor can go in a lot of different directions (some productive and others not so much). What I want to get worked out in a technical review is as follows:

- Overall technology stack – This is important as it gives me an indication of how current the technology is as well as whether we like the overall technical direction of the vendor. Some firms have very strict standards on the languages and platforms that are used and others seem more agnostic as long as they think the overall technology direction is reasonable. A vendor's technology and future direction are indicators of the investment the firm is making in the software and their commitment to investing in the platform into the future.

- Scalability and associated hardware/hosting – Understand the hardware and/or hosting costs associated with running the application given your current and future production volumes. There are two parts to the question: a.) can the system process my business problem in the business timeframes necessary, and b.) what is the cost of the resources to support the scale that I need. For prospective clients with large processing volumes, how many vendors express concern over their ability to process it effectively? Typically, they say 'Oh yeah, it can handle it' and then go on and talk about their threading model or some other scalability features. If you are bigger than the vendor's biggest client this may not be a problem, but you are going to want to move this risk up on your project plan to confirm that it truly isn't an issue.

- Data access / integration options – I have this third on this list but from a practical standpoint can be very important and is often overlooked. The core question here is how friendly is the software to allowing me to load or extract data from the system, typically on a bulk basis. Systems that are considered 'open' have features that allow for ease of integration and extendibility. Systems that do not have open APIs, download features, etc. can make it very difficult for a firm to integrate the solution with other solutions within the client's overall software architecture.

- Security – Particularly for products that are going to operate outside of your corporate infrastructure, due diligence on the security of the system is important not only to protect the integrity of your data but also because there may be regulatory and compliance considerations as well.

It is worth noting that your firm may or may not have the skillset to do this type of technical evaluation. If you don't have this skillset, it may make sense to work with a consultant to help you evaluate.

Vendor Stability/Viability

Doing research on publicly traded vendors is a pretty straight forward exercise but for smaller, privately owned vendors it is a little more difficult and likely more of a risk/concern. Prospective clients wanted to get some level of comfort that our firm was viable and not at risk of going out of business. The solution we used with good success was to provide to a finalist prospect's Chief Financial (or Technology) Officer a confidential 3-year summary balance sheet and income statement on the business. As a private company, we were reluctant to release this information but understood it was an important element of the due diligence process. This seemed to work well as it provided them insight into our financial health but also provided us limited dissemination of this information.

References

It is typical for a prospect to ask a vendor for several client references that they can speak with as part of their overall vendor selection due diligence. References are a great way to learn about hands-on experiences with the vendor, specifically in the areas of overall customer service and support. With that being said, there are a few guidelines regarding references that I think are important to follow:

- Remember that a reference is a vendor's client doing them a favor by talking to you. As a vendor, I did not want to wear out my welcome with clients providing references and to that end, I only wanted references done if the prospective client was in their final due diligent steps. If you are not running references on your finalist vendor, then you should not be running the references. It is similar to hiring an employee – you run references as a final step – not on all the candidates.

- Honor the vendor's desire to make introductions or facilitate scheduling of the reference. Don't ever call a reference provided by a vendor without notifying them first. The exception to this is if you have your own reference sources – that is, you know people at firms that you can call on your own.

Total Cost of Ownership

I have worked with many firms who require that a Total Cost of Ownership Analysis be performed on the vendors being evaluated. The analysis is designed to expose the total costs of the project and give an 'all-in' cost across the different vendors. This is a good approach because without it, the vendors are often being compared by just licensing costs and this can be misleading for comparison purposes. Aside from the comparison benefit, the real benefit of this analysis is that it provides a full understanding of how a vendor works and the potential escalation in costs that may occur over time. By analyzing all the cash flow factors, you get a clear understanding of the business model of a vendor. Total Cost of Ownership should also be embraced if your firm is considering a build. Internal technology groups are notorious for underestimating the total cost of building and maintaining a system and often just focus on the initial development costs which can be just the tip of the iceberg.

Things to consider in your analysis:

- Licensing, Subscription, Maintenance Costs – Costs for using the software over time – you will find a lot more discussion on this in chapter 3.

- Implementation Services – Costs paid to vendor and/or third-party consultants.

- Hardware/Hosting Costs – Hardware if you are hosting and hosting costs if being outsourced.

- Staffing costs – Internal staffing that may increase or decrease based on needs of the software.

Trials

A software trial is a firm's ability to use an application for a specific period before they commit to licensing the application. Some vendors will do this and some will not. Hosted applications with little data integration needs often have an easier time doing a trial than an installed/integrated product. As a vendor, I do not like trials for the following reasons:

- Your acceptance/warranty is essentially a trial. Yes, you do have to execute a contract and that takes legal effort, but the agreement gives you an out if you determine that the application is not a fit. Pick the best vendor and roll with them – if you did a good job during your due diligence you should be in good shape.

- Trials normally require a commitment of training, a learning curve, etc. and leaving a client to their own devices to make a decision on the application that they are just learning doesn't make sense. The 'let our team just play with it' is typically not a winning plan. Don't be surprised if a vendor agrees to the trial, but only if the time dedicated to it is billable.

Selecting the Final Vendor

You have gone through the selection process and have a lot of meaty information from the vendors, their capabilities, pricing, etc. Hopefully you have learned a lot about your own organization and how you can improve it with a new software solution. We have talked about many of the key elements of the evaluation process and now it is time to pick the best solution. I am not going to suggest any grading or weighting system for picking the final vendor – that is up to you. I will, however, make some suggestions that will serve well as your firm proceeds:

- **Overall pick is the firm's selection** – not technology, not business but a collective decision. You want to avoid a situation in the future where a group is saying, 'If we had picked our choice then we would not be having these issues'. You need buy-in from all parties as they are all going to be important during the implementation process.

- **Executive Support/Expectations** – Be clear on what problems the new solution is going to solve and provide clarity on what it is not going to do. The firm is making an investment and it is important they are clear on the anticipated return on that investment.

- **Is doing nothing the best solution?** What if you are underwhelmed by the offerings? Firms feel like they must pick the solution that fits best and that may well be a good choice. Just remember that you have the option of picking nothing and sometimes it becomes clear during the evaluation process that standing pat may be the best overall business decision.

Buyer Remorse – Why the Wrong System Gets Picked

It is hard to quantify whether a firm has bought the 'best' system for their needs and it is often the case that multiple software systems would serve a client well. With that being said, firms do pick systems that really are not a good fit for their goals. These situations seem to occur when the following scenarios come into play:

- Buyer does not fully understand the problem they are trying to solve. The buyer has unrealistic expectations or undisclosed needs that are not explored during the evaluation process. I have heard buyers say, 'It seemed great in the demo but it doesn't do what we expected'. Of course, the software demo was good – vendors spend a lot of time working on making their software show well. As the buyer, it is your job to dig beyond the slick demo and determine if it is a good fit for your business. Remember that the devil is in the details and it may be less obvious deficiencies that have a significant negative impact on a system's ability to fit your needs.

- Avoid the beauty contest – several years back we spent a bunch of money 'freshening' the look of our interface to make the product look more current. This project provided our clients no functional value but we were getting feedback that our UI was looking 'dated'. In the world of web interfaces, look and feel matters a lot more than it did back when most apps had standard Windows interfaces. The look of an interface can be an indicator of how modern the application is but more often users just have a propensity to lean towards prettier software. Users also love other visualizations such as animated or exploding graphs, etc. These are all fine things but don't ignore your core business needs at the expense of these bright sparkly things.

- Personal/Corporate Relationship – Relationships can impact a selection process. Examples:

    o Project sponsor went to college with the product manager at a specific vendor.

    o Client already has a relationship with a specific vendor and wants to consolidate all software with that vendor.

These may be perfectly reasonable reasons to go with a vendor but if the only reason, then you are rolling the dice on whether it is the best solution for your firm.

🃏 Chicken Wings

I love chicken wings. Love them. They are inexpensive, delicious, and can be prepared in so many glorious ways. In the infamous words of Chris Farley in the movie Tommy Boy[12]:

> Boy, some chicken wings would really hit the spot.

> Tommy likey! Tommy wants wingey!

Bone-in wings? Of course – boneless are not wings – they are tenders – which is a completely different thing. I'm down with a good plate of tenders – they just aren't wings. Why am I talking about chicken wings?

Here's why.

When you are traveling, you should be able to get a good plate of wings in pretty much any airport or city that you are traveling in. But this is not the case. You are tired from travel, sick of wearing a suit, and just need an emotional pick-me-up. A good plate of wings and I am back in the game! I'm shocked by how many places can botch the preparation of chicken wings. If I were to open a restaurant, the first thing I would do is make sure I have epic wings on the menu. So, I provide some guidance on wing preparation to restaurants near and far.

- **Undercooked/Slimy Wings** – biggest no-no. Just gross and unforgiveable. I ask for my wings to be cooked 'well done' or 'extra crispy' specifically to avoid the slimy factor. If there is ever a question of whether they are cooked enough then cook them some more. I don't even like to say the word slimy – makes me shiver.

- **Broken Bone Wings** – Yuck. I don't want to get a bite of bone fragments – this makes me not want to eat any more. I will concede that occasionally there will be a broken one, however there should never be more than one on a plate and only then it should be the occasional outlier. I think this happens when they are cutting them up. Notice to cutter – if you break one then throw in the trash as a casualty – do not put in the bucket of wings to be cooked. Interestingly, I am not bothered by an errant feather left on my wing. You would think that this would be an issue after my broken bone rant but just doesn't invoke the same reaction.

- **Crappy Sauce Wings** – Wings are great plain. Drop them in the fryolator, crisp them up, grind a bit of course salt and you are good to go. But then you go and dip them in something like Auntie Sue's secret recipe sauce and it is just bad now. You ruined some otherwise yummy wings. There are many different wing sauces but the most common is the classic Buffalo sauce. You know it is essentially hot sauce, butter, and vinegar, right? It's not hard to make. There are some terrific wing sauces out there but be honest with yourself and if your sauce is gross then don't soak my wings in it or go with a simple Buffalo sauce and all will be good.

- **Breaded then Sauced = Soggy Wings** – You made a nice crispy wing and you decided that you wanted to bread it first. I have no issue with this and crispy breading can be a tasty option. However, you cannot then go and make that nice crispiness a soggy mess by dipping in a sauce. It totally defeats the purpose. Do your nice crispy breaded wing, but put sauce on the side. One exception here may be a sticky/non-watery sauce (such as a honey habanero) that coats the breading instead of soaking it up. I will leave you to decide but the key is it must stay crispy! Another great idea I have encountered occasionally – mix the sauce and the breading and affix to wing BEFORE putting in fryolator – then you get a spicy crispy coating on the wing – solid effort!

- **Monstrous Wings** – Bigger is not better in wings. Tiny is not good either but I will take small over huge wings. Get regular size wings – big enough to have some meat on them but small enough that they don't look like genetic mutants. A side problem with huge wings is that they take longer to cook so they have a better chance at slimy which we have established is the first sin of wings.

- **Dipping Sauce** – A good wing should not need to be dipped in a secondary sauce – it should stand on its own. However, I, like many of you, like to dip my Buffalo wings in blue cheese. Ranch dressing is a little disappointing but depending on the wing recipe can be an acceptable alternative. Charging me extra for blue cheese seems a little harsh but I'm happy to pay provided it is good chunky blue cheese and not some crappy thin facsimile of the real thing.

- **Whole or Pieces** – Most places cut their wings into the 'wingy' and 'dingy' (little drumstick) parts and discard the wing tip. Others will serve all three parts together as a unit. Baked wings (not done in fryolator) are often done as a whole and are great if you can find someone who can do a proper baked wing but that seems to be harder to find than an acceptable fried wing. The concept of whole vs. pieces also confuses the wing count. If your menu says that you get 6 wings in an order – is that 6 pieces or is that 6 whole wings? An important consideration if you are evaluating the proper size for your current wing hunger. I think there should be some standards around this and that a wing is considered the wingy and dingy together – cutting it in half doesn't make it two wings – it makes it two halves which is still just one wing.

- **Alternative/Imposter Wings** – Chickens are not the only birds out there with wings (does a bird, by definition, have wings?). At Thanksgiving, there are two turkey wings. I always think that someone else is going to take them but they are always available – everyone goes for the boring white meat. The turkey wingy is great and a highly-ignored item. You will see duck wings on menus but normally they are not wings – they are actually drumsticks – and not the dingy part of the wing – an actual drumstick (leg). They are generally delicious but not really wings. Just the other day, I saw pork wings on a menu and this is not the first time. A pork 'wing' is often a pork shank or some sort of rib meat tip that is put in sauce to suggest a wing. Ever heard the expression 'when pigs fly'? It is because pigs don't have wings and although the offering may be delightful – it is not a wing.

- **The Unexpected Wing** – You go to a nice restaurant and look at the menu and will probably go with a nice steak or piece of fish. Your healthy-eating wife orders the roasted chicken. Meals come and everyone is enjoying their food and then it happens. She only eats the white meat so being handed to you is one happy little chicken wing cut from the side of her chicken. A chicken wing bonus! They say life is about the little things – here is proof.

- **Wet-Wipes/Post Wing Cleanup** – I get right in there and enjoy my wings – no utensils – that would be strange. I have been known to make a little mess while eating them but once I am done I want the plate gone and want to clean up. Wet-wipes are important and I encourage providing them but recently a place brought me lemon water and a little towel – that was the Rolls Royce of wing cleanup!

I don't claim to speak for all the world's wing eating population but I think if wing creators follow these principles, you will please most of us.

Chapter 3: Finances of Software

I wish I had a silver bullet that I could share with readers about how to get the best deal on purchasing your enterprise software and related services. Mister Crabs in SpongeBob SquarePants[13] had the venerable Crabby Patty Recipe as his silver bullet for making piles of money but in our world, it is not so easy. I have however seen a lot of different deals get done and have found that many people involved in the process don't understand the different options potentially available to them. As a vendor, I always said that I wanted to get fair value for our software so we could effectively run our business and have the resources to service our clients – the actual structure of the deal could go several different ways. My goal in this section is to discuss a.) the typical way software deals are structured, and b.) the motivations of vendors and buyers for structuring different ways. I am going to use some metrics in this section that I have encountered in the financial services industry; I will leave to you to determine if they are applicable in other industries.

Perpetual vs. Subscription (Term)

If you want to get a new car, you essentially have two choices: Buy or Lease. A perpetual software license is like the 'Buy' – you pay for the whole thing up front (we aren't going to talk about financing your car – it doesn't fit the analogy). A subscription or term license is like the 'Lease' – you get to use the software for a certain amount of time. A perpetual license often has a second annual 'Support/Maintenance' component broken out as well. Some companies will only quote one or the other, with subscriptions being more prevalent today, however most vendors have a formula for converting from one to the other. I have seen deals that are sort of hybrids of the two types as well – there is plenty of room for creativity.

A simple example:

Perpetual:

> License: $100k
>
> Maintenance: $20k/year (20% of original license)

Subscription:

> Annual Subscription: $40k/year
>
> Maintenance: None (built into the Subscription fee – not always the case though)

Note: We converted our perpetual license to subscription by using the simple formula: **(license amount) / 2.5** (a simple but conventional conversion methodology)

For the two options, below is the 5 year amounts that you would pay for each:

5 Year Cash Flow[§]

Model	Yr1	Yr2	Yr3	Yr4	Yr5	Total
Perpetual	120	20	20	20	20	200
Subscription	40	40	40	40	40	200

[§] Finance people are gasping that we did not discount the cashflows so this is not a reasonable comparison! I know – we could have done that but then the total amount wouldn't match and the example would be mucked up. Still not happy? – Feel free to discount on your own using whatever discount rate you wish.

You can see in our simple model above that the total out of pocket cost is $200k for both, so which is better?

Which one is better depends on several variables, and more importantly who you ask, but the drivers can be interesting:

Buyer:

- Budgeting – Do I have $120k in the budget this year? In a lot of firms there is a 'use it or lose it' mentality on budgets. This buyer may have the money in the budget (or the firm has had a good year and wants to spend some cash in the current fiscal year) and sees this as a great opportunity to use the perpetual plan.

- Finance says that they like subscription because it is off-balance-sheet and they don't have to capitalize the software – they say I must go with the subscription.

- This software solution is a short-term fix for us – we will probably only run it for a few years and then go to another technology – the subscription will be more cost effective in this case. Alternatively, the firm plans on running the solution for the next decade – the perpetual is a better value.

Vendor:

- Software Salesperson – I need this deal to go perpetual because it fulfills my quota for the quarter – the subscription won't get me there.

- Software Executive - I want subscription deals because they build my recurring revenue base and that is what the market wants to see, which will help our stock price.

- Small Company CFO – Get me the perpetual deal – I need the cash flow now!

The point of the bullets above is to demonstrate that different people in the purchasing decision process have different motivations and goals that have nothing to do with the amount of the deal. Understanding these different motivations can help both parties come up with a final deal where they both win. Let's look at some other stuff that makes things a bit more complicated.

Understanding a Vendor's Pricing Model

Earlier we talked about comparing the perpetual vs. subscription options and admittedly used a highly-simplified pricing model to make the comparison. We are now going to discuss how un-simple a pricing model can become and the multiple factors that can go into it. Back when perpetual pricing was the norm, it was less important to understand these factors, but now that subscriptions are more prevalent, you need to understand the factors that are going into your annual subscription costs to help assess what your future costs could be. All the options below are designed in some way to either measure the client's usage or the vendor's costs (or both).

- Users – User Licensing or 'Seats' is a way for a vendor to limit the number of users who can use the software. This can be done two ways: Named Users or Concurrent Users. A named user takes up a user slot regardless of whether the user is ever logged into the system. Concurrent users are a bit more forgiving because it sets a limit to the number of users who can be using the system at the same time. You could have 100 named users and as long as no more than 10 people are logged in at any one time you would not exceed a 10-user concurrent license restriction. User is a highly-used metric to measure usage and therefore is often a good proxy for the amount of hardware that will be necessary to run the software for the client.

- Disk Storage – Seen more in a hosting/cloud environment, a vendor can charge for the disk storage that a client uses. This component has two key aspects: a.) allows the vendor to align their storage costs with your usage, and b.) can be an initiator to encourage archiving of historical data which can make the overall application more efficient.

- Network Traffic – Another metric that is more in a hosted/cloud environment measures the amount of bandwidth being used. Think about the data plan on your phone (and your kid's inability to stay within the allotted bandwidth) – it's like that.

- CPUs, Cores – A vendor may structure pricing based on the amount of processing horsepower necessary to run your business. Much like user based pricing, this is meant to be a reflection of usage. I have been involved with software that did this and buyers typically would respond 'why am I being penalized for running on faster hardware'. Fair point, but if you don't like user based pricing, we need to use some metric. In recent years, hardware virtualization has made this harder to implement as the resources can now be variable.

- Instances, Engines – Another measure of usage. Generally tied to the number of instances of the software or engines that are required for you to run your business. One key consideration here is whether this will require you to separately license TEST or UAT (User Acceptance Testing) licenses separately. If you don't know then ask because vendors are not always forthcoming about this additional cost.

- Quantity – Quantities are a metric of size. Measures such as the number of accounts and the amount of money being run on the system are measures of quantity. The financial services industry uses a metric called AUM (Assets Under Management) as a measure to indicate size. A typical personal financial planner may charge you 1% annually to manage your money – as your nest egg grows, so does the manager's fees. This is often referred to as basis point pricing (a basis point is equal to .01%). In above example, the manager is charging you 100 basis points.

- Transactions – Have you ever looked at the pricing sheet for your bank account? The bank can provide you an a la carte menu of fees you can pay. For example:

    o Domestic Wire – $35 per transaction

    o Checks $1 per transaction (beyond first 25)

    o Overdraft $50 per bounced check

  You get the idea. Not a metric I have seen used a lot in the pricing of enterprise software but another measure of usage.

- Tolerance for Pain – I saved the best for last. The tolerance for pain pricing methodology uses a completely different approach. The basis of it is 'how much can I get the client to pay me for the software'. The market is set by the collection of vendors and we need to determine how we fit into that matrix. Example: There are 5 vendors in the space and we know from market feedback that the annual prices range from $50 – 100k per year for the software. The market leader is not surprisingly the $100k vendor. We think that we are functionally competitive with them but do not have the name recognition that they do. We are therefore going to price at $80k. Oversimplified example? Yeah – maybe a little bit but not far from the truth – I have seen vendors use far crazier logic.

Pricing is challenging because you are trying to address all the below points but they don't always fit together nicely:

- I need my pricing model to protect me from my client's usage habits, therefore I want my largest cost exposures covered by the model.

- I want to participate in usage growth – If my client doubles in size, I want to get some revenue growth from that as well.

- I must deal with the reality of competitive pricing to sign new deals.

- I want to have a reasonable level of pricing integrity throughout my client base to protect against large pricing disparities across similar clients.

Term/Renewal

The term of an agreement indicates the number of years (or months, etc.) that a client is committed to paying for the software. If someone says 'it's a perpetual deal with a three-year maintenance agreement' it means that they will pay their $100k (from earlier example) and then is committed to paying the $20k/year for 3 years. Term is a double-edged sword for the buyer in that a longer term will force them to commit longer but also provides price certainty during that term. Remember that the vendor (generally) has the right to reprice a renewal agreement after the initial term so it is important to understand how that could be done. Three to five year terms seem to be the norm. One more thing - most subscriptions have an auto-renew concept – that is, if the buyer does not explicitly cancel then it is assumed that they want to renew for another period.

Escalators

I just talked about locking in your pricing within your term renewal period. Within that term there could be another pricing element called an escalator. The escalator is designed to provide an incremental increase in the user's fees within the term of the agreement. Escalators are typically based on a market rate such as CPI index, a flat percentage, or a combination of both. If I had an escalator 'CPI plus 1% starting in year 2' then to calculate my $40k subscription in the second year would require me to go look up the consumer price index (a standard rate used to measure inflation) – let's say .5%, so your year 2 subscription would be (1 + .01 +.005) * $40k = $40,600. Not a huge impact but compound for a few years and drive the CPI higher and you will see how the escalator can become relevant.

As a buyer, you may say: *'we will just negotiate the escalator out of the deal.'* Possibly – but one thing to consider is that the escalator may actually be a good thing. As a vendor, I didn't like to go back and re-negotiate on renewals. If we had a reasonable escalator, then we were good with letting our agreements auto-renew on an annual basis at the escalated rate. If we got beat up on the escalator when doing the contract, then we would use the renewal term as way to reprice.

Maintenance/Support

The term 'maintenance' is a general term that has some grey areas as to what it truly entails, however, I'm going to define maintenance as a.) the right to get future versions of the software, and b.) access to the vendor's support infrastructure to address critical bugs and questions. I have seen maintenance costs range from 10 to 25% of the core license with 15 to 20% the norm. Maintenance is a pretty standard construct, however there are variations within these agreements:

- Allotted support hours – some vendors have an 'all you can eat' policy on support while others allocate a designated number of hours that can be used on a quarterly or annual basis. Normally they have a "use 'em or loose 'em" policy. If you go over the allotted number of hours, then you pay consulting rates for the overage hours. Like many things, there are positives and negatives associated with it. Negative: Needs to be tracked, hours need to be determined if they fall into the support bucket or not. For example: If I report a bug and ask the vendor to confirm that it is a bug – should that go towards my hours? I have been on many a call where vendor and client disagree on this. Positive: Vendor gets cost certainty on support and although buyer does not have an all you can eat situation, they do have clarity on hours.

- Vendor pays for missing SLA – Plenty of clients' lawyers have language that says that if the vendor misses SLA (Service Level Agreements) then the vendor must pay a financial penalty for their lack of support. As a vendor, I never agreed to do this – I would rather leave the deal on the table than to have this term. It undermines the relationship and causes a lot of unnecessary tracking and ambiguities that can be very toxic. A big 'No' on this one for me.

Revenue Recognition

Revenue recognition is an important topic for vendors because it dictates when revenue can be counted in the firm's financial results. Large or public vendors will use an accrual (GAAP – Generally Accepted Accounting Principles in US) methodology which dictates when revenue can be recognized. Smaller vendors may use a simple cash accounting method (revenue is recognized when received).

I freely admit that I have nightmares about GAAP accounting – the rules make my head spin (and I make no representation of GAAP expertise in below examples). However, there are a few core concepts that I think are important to cover if you want to understand the motivations of a vendor. If I am a GAAP vendor and I need to generate some recognizable business before the end of the year, which of the two deals do I want?

- Perpetual deal for $400k signed and invoiced on Dec 30th.

- Subscription deal for $1 million signed on Dec 1st.

Answer: I want the perpetual deal because I can realize the whole thing this year (I would only get 1/12th of the subscription this year). Also – do not be surprised that the vendor is highly motivated to deliver the software and an invoice to you on New Year's Eve – part of the recognition rules.

Now, what if I am a cash accounting vendor - the motivations can be a little less clear. Short answer is that I probably want the subscription deal. I may also be deciding if I want to get paid this year or next year because assuming my fiscal year is calendar year – this could have a big impact on my earnings and ultimately the tax liability due in March. I could defer getting paid if that was beneficial. Don't be surprised if a smaller vendor is more interested in payment timing. It may be for cash flow reasons but more likely it is about profit/loss and tax consequences.

There are some other interesting revenue recognition items that I won't go into but the key point is that revenue recognition matters to vendors. They say that the best time to buy a car is at the end of a quarter – I asked the manager of a car dealership if this was true and he said, 'It depends on whether I need the deal to reach my quota on the quarter but – generally yes'. Quarter and year-ends are good for both buyers and sellers because it provides a deadline that both parties can use to their advantage. The buyer can probably leverage the deadline to get a better overall deal and the seller can use the deadline to get the deal completed – both parties win.

Putting 'the Screws to' the Vendor

Vendors are used to working with buyers who will use deadlines, etc. to their advantage to get the best pricing and as just discussed I think for the most part that this is good for both parties. However, there are situations where a buyer can push a vendor into a sub-market deal. I will salute you for your negotiating prowess, however consider the impact that this could have on your long-term relationship with the vendor. Vendors are like elephants – they don't forget. I once had a large client negotiating a deal with me and he actually wanted to change the later-year terms of the deal to be higher because he said if he didn't they would become financially irrelevant as a client. I'm not suggesting that you just decide to pay more but I thought this was a very insightful observation by the buyer. Negotiation is a healthy part of the software acquisition process but remember that the vendor's long term health is in your best interests and the terms of your deal can set the groundwork (good or bad) for your future relationship.

Modules

'What do you mean I didn't get that piece of software – you showed it to me in the demo'? Just because you saw it in the demo doesn't mean you licensed everything you saw. Enterprise software often comes in modules and overall this is a pretty good thing because you can just pay for the stuff that you need. Just be clear on what you are getting and what you are not and if not clear, have your sales person itemize what is and is not included in the deal.

Buying Services - T&M vs. Fixed Price

How should I structure/pay for my software development or integration services? T&M (Time and Materials) is essentially paying on an hourly basis and Fixed Price is exactly what it sounds like: Paying for something at an agreed upon price.

The conventional wisdom generally goes that the vendor/developer of the software wants to do T&M and the buyer would generally prefer Fixed Price to limit their risk of cost overruns. Seems simple but below is some practical color on the topic that I think both parties should think about when considering how things should work.

I have not done many fixed price projects but I have done some. Different firms have varying philosophies on fixed price deals. For me to consider fix pricing a project, I need to:

a.) believe I fundamentally know the requirements of what needs to be built so I can estimate accurately,

b.) know the requirements of the project are not going to 'evolve' (also known as creep),

c.) anticipate I can build it for less than the cost of the estimate, or

d.) have a special reason that I will fix price:

- I want to build it and have the functionality so I am looking for someone to help underwrite the development.

- I have resources on the shelf that I need to get generating some cash flow.

- We have opportunity to sign a new client with whom we want to establish a long-term relationship and don't want risk being over budget.

The practical problems:

For a project with any level of complexity, the requirements or function points of a project should be documented so there is a record of what needs to be built and estimated. Some firms are quite good at doing this analysis but the majority are not. Even if you are great at writing specs, the needs of a project change/evolve as you get into it – this is not a bad thing – it is actually positive because the end product will likely be better than originally specified. BUT – what about the cost – who should pay for this creative morphing of the product?

In a T&M scenario, the vendor basically says, 'I'll do whatever you want because you are paying me for whatever I do'. In a fixed price arrangement, the vendor says, 'This is not in the original spec – we are going to have to re-estimate'. Unfortunately, it gets a bit murkier from here.

- Buyer – it is not in the original spec but it is 'implied'

- Buyer – it is not in the original spec but the way we are suggesting is actually easier

- Vendor – we would have designed differently if we had known of this – it is going to be a big change

On a Fixed Price contract, there is normally a 'change management' form that each party is supposed to sign and agree to any change in functionality and the price change associated with it.   In my experience, this form is often skipped.

Example: Challenging project on fixed price agreement:

- Buyer says it is just a simple change – can you slip it in. Vendor – Ok

- Vendor is running over on allocated hours so starts trying to de-scope or simplify other components of the project to make up some and finds themselves increasingly saying – 'it's not in scope'

- Buyer gets annoyed that yes, it is in scope and it is in spec

- Vendor says it is in spec but not the way it is being described

- Vendor is over budget but has little recourse so does whatever they can do to get it wrapped up

- Vendor feels hostage to project because can't get final payment until buyer signs off on completion

The same project on a T&M path:

- Buyer wants to make changes – Vendor says no problem

- Vendor has no problem building things however anyone at buyer directs

- Buyer gets invoices and says, 'we are burning through a lot of budget' – are we on schedule/budget? Vendors says no because your people keep changing things

- Buyer says – why did it take so long to code that thing? – it should have been straightforward

- Buyer reaches budget limit but project is not done. Vendor expects buyer to keep paying and explains to buyer that it is their fault for changing scope, requirements, etc.

- Buyer puts the clamps on

What about 'Not to Exceed'?

A Not to Exceed arrangement conceptually says, 'You can bill me up to x amount but if the project comes in at less than x then you will only bill me the hours that were necessary.'   At first glance this seems like a great deal for the buyer because it provides a cap on how much they will spend but also provides the potential for a lower price. In practice, a Not to Exceed deal is typically just a T&M deal that has a cap on it unless it is specifically written that all services will be delivered under the cap. More likely the language will say that the vendor will not go over without approval of the buyer. From a practical standpoint, the Not to Exceed amount is often the amount of spend that has been approved for a vendor and puts the onus on the vendor to stop billing the client at that point without some further action. Bottom line: a Not to Exceed deal can feel more like a T&M deal or Fixed Price deal depending on how the language is specifically written and it is important for buyer and vendor to have a clear understanding of this going into the agreement.

They Bill Me for Everything

Vendors/consultants like to invoice clients for time spent on their account. It can be an important source of revenue for them and the managers who run these teams are likely incented one way or another on their billings. Below are situations where the vendor and the client often look differently at what should be billed:

- Support or Implementation – Many vendors will bill for implementation resources and not for support resources. Be clear on who you are calling and the terms associated with that service. If you are calling the help line you will likely not be billed or it will be counted against your allotted support hours. If you are calling your implementation team – expect to be billed.

- Bug or User Error – If a client calls with an issue and it turns out that the issue is due to a bug in the software – should they be billed for that time? Probably not. What if the client calls with what they think is a bug and the vendor researches and figures out that the client used an unapproved method to change data in the application database causing a data corruption. Should the client be billed for that time? Probably. These are two relatively straightforward examples but there is gray area in between. It normally boils down to who is responsible for the cause of the issue.

- Work or Rework – A client requests that work be performed by the vendor. The vendor performs the work and 30 days later the client reports that there is an issue with the work performed. Did the vendor make a mistake or did the client discover a use case that wasn't covered in the initial design? Situations like this require judgement calls but expect a vendor to lean to the side of billing.

Have a conversation with the vendor about how they deal with the above situations and what you should expect to be billed for. That you are having the conversation with the vendor will sensitize them to the fact that you are monitoring these situations.

Some clients are very sensitive to unexpected invoices and others are not. If you do not want unexpected invoice surprises, below are a few ideas on some rules you can establish with your vendor:

- Get pre-approval if greater than x hours. This can become an administrative hassle but if x is some reasonable number then it can be helpful.

- Work must be performed on a work order – This is another pre-approval technique. Some clients will do a 'miscellaneous' work order that says something like 'Bill me up to 50 hours for support related work'. This provides a cap on your spending and allows you to track against this limit.

- More invoice detail/transparency on tasks performed – Some vendors provide a high level of detail on invoices but most do not. If you do not understand what you are being invoiced for then ask for clarity.

- Rules on who can request/approve work – Be clear on who can approve work – is it anyone at the client or does it need to be approved by an authorized approver? If it is not clear, a vendor will perform requested work and expect to be paid.

The above all seem like reasonable items but a word of caution. The more difficult/cumbersome you make it for a vendor to get paid and perform work for you, the more difficult it is going to be to get help. Understand that there are other clients who are willing to pay for premium service and access to resources.

Signing a Contract

I am not a lawyer and I didn't stay at a Holiday Inn Express last night however, I have worked on a lot of software contracts so will make some general observations that have served me well in the contract process.

Which Party Generates the First Draft of the Agreement?

Whose agreement are we going to use? Parties like to use their own agreements because they are familiar with the language and will require less change (because they wrote it the way they want it). If it is a software agreement, the vendor's agreement is most always used because the buyer does not have a licensing agreement and does not want to draft one from scratch. Large clients often do have a services agreement that they prefer over a vendor's agreement. We would often agree to using a client's agreement as a starting point because a.) they said we had no choice, and b.) it was easier to get the agreement completed so we could start doing work.

Matters of Business/Matters of Law

As I read through a software contract, I try and classify items as either a business item or a legal item. If it is a business item, then the terms of that business item should be in a deal sheet that I have agreed to with the client. A term (deal) sheet is a summary of business terms that make up the framework of a deal that an attorney can use to build out a full contract. If something is a matter of business, I feel it is my responsibility to get the terms worked out with the client before getting attorneys involved. The other nice thing about a term sheet is that it is much more condensed and easier to read for both parties. All other things in the contract I lump under Matters of Law – items that the lawyers can work on.

Matters of Business

Below is a list of items that are matters of business. Each contract can be different but getting these core items will go a long way to getting a contract drafted.

- Cashflows (license, subscription, maintenance)

- Length of Agreement

- Service Levels

- Acceptance

- Modules

- Site Designation

- User Limitations

Matters of Law

Matters of law are items that both buyers and sellers will negotiate to afford themselves protections in the relationship. My experience is that both buyers and sellers have pre-determined terms in these areas that they are looking to get in place. When dealing with large firms it is interesting that you are often working with legal assistants who have negotiating cheat sheets. These allow them to negotiate terms to a certain level but if the other party wants to go further, then an attorney needs to get involved.

If you see these terms, then you are dealing with matters of law:

- Indemnity

- Warranties

- Liability

- Infringement

- Intellectual Ownership

- Confidentiality

- Escrow

- Insurance Requirements

'It's in Legal'

Getting a contract completed can be a straightforward exercise but it normally is not. Particularly if you have two big firms working on a contract; it can take months to get it completed. I have heard 'It's in Legal' many times and my experience is that it is in some black hole waiting to be read. If you are a vendor, time is not on your side – a lot more bad can happen than good during this waiting period. It can help to work some incentives or deadlines into your term sheet on getting the agreement executed by a certain date to help move the agreement along. Buyers can also use the 'in legal' designation to buy themselves more time in the decision-making process. If you have not gotten a redline back from them after a long delay, assume that it is not yet in the queue for review. A key reason for this is often that the vendor was selected but the official dollars have not yet been approved. Sometimes it is just red tape and sometimes not but long delays in legal are typically a sign that something more concerning is causing the delay.

🃏 Embrace the Red Eye

I understand people's dislike of taking the red eye – it is no fun sitting (much less sleeping) on a plane. The alternative is crappy too though because you need to burn a whole day sitting there and you lose the day to travel. I decided I would embrace the red eye and make it my friend. After some practice, I have gotten pretty good at it and so I will share my 'red eye for success' tips:

- **Flatulence** - I'm not sure that this is a tip, but it's funny. In 2013, an article was published in the New Zealand Journal of Medicine, "Flatulence on Airplanes: Just Let It Go"[14]. The article basically says that flying increases gas but holding it in can have negative medical consequences so let your flatulence fly. I have had some experience with this situation (both on the giving and receiving end) but the funniest thing is that people wearing headphones should realize that just because their headphones are keeping them from hearing their business doesn't mean that we all can't dial in on what is going on. So, next time you are on a flight and trying to sneak one out, don't feel guilty, there are medical experts in your corner saying it is ok.

- **Window Seat** – I know plenty of people who prefer the aisle seat because they can get up without bothering the people next to them. Not on the red eye – go to the bathroom when you get on and then get into your window seat. Remember in the Wedding Singer[15] when Jules' elbow gets wacked by the drink cart – not satisfying. Not only do you want to get a window but you want the right or left side depending on what side you lean-sleep better. I'm not sure lean-sleep is a real term but you know what I mean – do you lean and sleep better to the left or to the right? For me, it is to the right – not sure why this is. You will have to experiment, but find your preferred side. You will also need a sweatshirt, jacket or something with a little fluffiness that you can ball up and lean into like a pillow.

- **Hat/Blanket. Glasses Off** – Find a blanket if you can (most red eyes have them). Those little pillows are ok but the blanket is the key. If you wear glasses take them off – put in the seat pouch so you can find them later. Some people like those eye masks to make it dark – I like a baseball hat that I can pull down over my eyes.

- **Sucky Sleep is Better Than No Sleep** – Go to sleep immediately. This is key. None of this 'I'm going to stay up for a while and read or watch a movie'. Glasses off, hat pulled down, warm blanket, lean into your fluffy sweatshirt and force yourself to sleep. Let's agree that you are not going to get a great night's sleep but that is not what you need. It may not feel like you are sleeping but you are getting sleep benefit. After a few hours of crappy sleep, you are just uncomfortable. Time to change positions. Time for the head down on the seat tray. This is not optimal but it does get your body in a different position (assuming you are short enough to stuff your head down there behind the seat in front of you). I once had this going and the person in front of me pushed their seat recline and squashed my head – be careful! You need to get enough crappy sleep so that you are functional the following day. If you are not functional the following day, then it sort of defeats the purpose of flying the red eye in the first place.

- **Booze** – Have a nice dinner and a few drinks if that is good for you but if you drink too much a.) you are going to have to go to the bathroom and having to go from your window seat annoys the people next to you, and b.) you risk being hung over which does not mix well with crappy sleep.

- **Drugs** – I know people who take 'sleeping aids' before they get on the red eye. I'm not sure how legal they always are but I consider this cheating. I'm not judging – I just don't like pills - so not in my routine.

- **Teeth Brushing Alternatives** – You wake up from your crappy sleep, it is probably dark or just getting light out and they flip the cabin lights on. Time to feel human again. Assuming that you are not going to brush your teeth (you have no place to spit your toothpaste), you need to be carrying a Listerine Pocketmist (squirter) and/or a box of Altoids. I like the Listerine – 4 or 5 squirts and you are rocking the minty freshness like Donkey in Shrek. Chomping on a handful of Altoids works well too. They make those weird breath strips that dissolve in your mouth – those are strange – skip those. Bonus! The unnaturally happy flight attendant just brought me a hot towel! She needs to use tongs to give it to me because It just came out of the microwave and it is about 1000 degrees but I love those - right on the face! – ahhh. If you don't get a hot towel, you can bring your own alcohol wipe but it is not the same.

So, there you have it. You need to get your preparation and expectations right to be a good red eye flyer. Have a good attitude, the right tools, and get some crappy sleep so you are functional for the whole next day (hopefully fishing but working if you must) – great job!

I'm Not Technical But ...

I wish I had a nickel for each time I have heard a non-technical person say:

I'm not technical but ...

- That estimate is way too high

- It should be running faster

- I think that should be easy to fix

I think that these folks should a.) learn something about technology, or b.) stop saying it. Probably a little harsh, but by premising your statement with 'non-technical' you are essentially saying that you are not qualified to make the comment but you are going to make it anyways. I get it – you want the estimate lower, the software to be faster, etc.

Based on the following scale, if you are below a 3, then consider suppressing your technical opinions. If you are a 3 or higher, you don't have to say: 'I'm not technical' because you now have some technical qualifications!

1   Operate a web browser, send email, and probably write a basic Word document or Excel spreadsheet. Excellent online shopper.

2   Can use all components of Office, able to do formatting, and other features and probably know some additional software applications as well such as QuickBooks, TurboTax, etc. They do not intimidate me.

3   In addition to above, I know how a web application works, have done some SQL, scripting/macro-writing. If I took apart a PC, I could identify the main pieces inside the case.

4   I consider myself a programmer and not only can I program but have some understanding of networking, software design principals, database administration, etc.

5   I know multiple languages, design patterns, and my job generally entails telling other programmers how things should be done.

6   I'm a technology rock star – you wouldn't understand what I do even if I explained it.

Technical knowledge for a non-developer is powerful. If you are in sales, you get instant credibility if you have product knowledge and technical chops – it differentiates you and enables you to sell more software. Don't let the techies get the satisfaction of talking over your head.

Top things a non-technical person should do

The below items are not particularly complicated and you can find a host of tutorials and resources online. If I walk by your desk and see you on CNN, I grumble about you wasting time but if I see you on an html style sheet tutorial, I praise your quest for learning. Be that person.

- Create an html page in notepad with text image and dropdown. Add style tags to make it look good. Open in a browser and keep changing.

- SQL primer – Create a database, create tables, select/insert/update/delete, procedures/functions, joins, etc. If you go through the first 5 chapters of any SQL book, you will learn the basics.

- Excel macros – VB is part of Excel. It is a full-blown programming language. Do some tutorials and you will learn some cool Excel stuff and probably learn that there are ways to automate tasks that you used to do manually. Do you know how to use functions, named ranges, crosstabs, and other more advanced features? Don't be afraid – it is fun.

- Program (VB, Java, C#) – Pick a language – your choice and learn

    o   Loops

    o   Variables

o   Arrays

o   Error handling

You are going to struggle with the syntax a bit – that is normal – push through it. The techies want you to give up but you are tougher than that!

- Read tech books/articles

    o   How the web actually works (TCP/IP, web servers, html, etc.)

    o   Basic networking

    o   Object-oriented programming fundamentals

    o   JavaScript and how to make web pages dynamic

    o   XML/JSON primer – what it is and why it is useful

You don't have to memorize everything – there is no quiz. By reading, you will pick up an understanding and over time the technical world just becomes clearer. I'm assuming that you don't want to be a programmer for a living but knowing this stuff makes you better at whatever job you do.

Chapter 4: Implementing Your New System

A Thousand Problems Await You

In the movie, Apollo 13[16], Jim Lovell says after finding out that there is a problem with their spacecraft, '*All right, there's a thousand things that have to happen, in order* [to bring the ship back to earth]. *We are on number eight.*'

Implementing software is hard. Not 'putting a man on the moon' hard but generally a challenging adventure. One of the key things that needs to be acknowledged up front is that there are going to be problems, issues, and changes that need to be made along the way and although your goal is to minimize them, accept the fact that it comes with the territory:

- It's ok – there are going to be problems – factor it into your budget and schedules.

- Do you have an efficient process for solving for the unexpected so they don't become bottlenecks?

- Keep positive – each solved problem gets you closer to the end!

Model Office

I first heard the term model office about 20 years ago, while working with a large investment bank who was evaluating a new software system. The firm had put together a collection of about 30 test cases that they said were the basis for the model office that they planned on running against the software. The interesting part of the test cases was that they were very specific test scenarios with actual numbers and the results that they expected to validate from the system. In the first step in the process, I sat with an analyst from the company and we spent two days stepping through the software on exactly how we would handle the test cases. This process was to determine 'if' we could handle the scenarios and to expose any functional gaps that may exist. The second phase of the model office was the client getting its end users involved and walking them through the scenarios with an emphasis on workflow. The 'if' had already been worked out so now they could focus on the 'how' and get feedback and validation from the users on whether the solution would work well for them.

I remember being incredibly impressed by this process for a few key reasons:

- The model office script was well thought out and detailed. It took a lot of effort to produce but it provided a clear roadmap of what they needed to accomplish and how they wanted to accomplish it.

- The users were engaged in the process and it gave them a clear understanding of where they were positioned from a functional risk standpoint as well having clarity on how their future workflow would be.

I have worked to embrace the concept of model office in the software implementation cycle since then and have found that although the approach often needs to be molded for different software and clients, the benefits continue to be high. The term 'model office' may get somewhat bastardized to fit the specific needs of a client but I think that is ok as long as it is focused on providing early understanding and exposure of project risk. Below are some different interpretations of model office that have evolved on various projects:

- The first month of the implementation is called model office and it is focused on users learning the software and prototyping how the system will ultimately be used or implemented. This work may be considered 'throw away' because we want people to be creative and learn what the opportunities are before having to build something that is going to go into production.

- The first milestone in the project is called model office and its goal is to deliver the first piece of functionality that will provide value to the business.

- Model office happens before the project officially starts. It is focused on workflows and use cases and establishing a full operational understanding of how the software will solve the firm's challenges. Not a coincidence that this takes place within the warranty period.

Excuses for skipping model office:

- **It's not in the budget or timeframe** – Except on very simple projects I would argue that you are going to have to do the model office tasks anyways – you are just going to do them later in the project. Exercising the system early in the process makes you ask questions and ultimately exposes issues that you want to find as soon as possible. Having a model office element to your project should help your plan and ultimately your budget.

- **We need to essentially implement the product before we can do it effectively** – This can be true for some projects but I'd say for most it is not a valid argument. Be a little creative and find ways to capture the spirit of model office even if it isn't 100% the way you would like it.

- **Our users don't have the time** – This is a leadership issue. Most projects don't end well when the user base is not involved in the process. The business sponsor of the project should consider the ramifications of a project that does not have their team's input. I'm not going to dispute that you can make more progress early on without the input of 'those annoying users' but think about whether it is really progress if you have to be reworking a lot of things once the users are engaged.

Get the A-Team

Remember the A-Team[17] from the 80's with Mr. T (*Pity the fool*)?   It wasn't CHiPs[18] good, but it was a pretty solid show.   I'm not talking about that A-Team though – I'm talking about the people who are going to make your project successful.   If I could pick only one success factor in getting your project to a happy place, it would be getting a talented team with the necessary skills to get the job done.   You need an A-team of smart and motivated people.   This seems like a pretty obvious point but it is actually a top reason that projects fail.   In a perfect world, I want the following:

- **Dedicated resources** – There are several initiatives going on so we can only give you 40% of Mary's time. This means that I get her two days a week. What if her other project needs more time? Does my project have to wait on her? Mary probably doesn't like it either because she has two project managers asking her when two different things are going to be done – unclear on how to prioritize and stresses her out.   I want dedicated resources that I know I can count on and have their full attention to the project. I understand that this is not always feasible but I do know that splitting resources is generally not efficient and most employees don't like it.

- **No fluff resources** – I don't want numbers of resources – I want talented resources. Fluff resources burn my budget and provide me little (or negative) productivity. I want the doers – the people who can do stuff. On average, I think about 75% of the critical work on a project is done by about 25% of the staff. Here are the skills I generally want:

- Product knowledge – People who know (or will quickly learn) the application that we are implementing. I'm amazed by how some people can learn a software application very quickly and others just can't. There are sponges and screens:

    - Sponge – They go through training, tutorials, or documentation and just get it. They understand the problem and are on a quest to master the software at hand.

    - Screen – They go through training, tutorials, or documentation and just don't get it. It's as if the knowledge passes right through them (like a screen). I think the foundation of this (or lack of foundation) is that they do not understand the purpose of the software and generally are not interested or motivated to be an expert.

    I want people with a track record of being a sponge on other projects.

- **Knowledge of the workflows and business logic** at the firm we are implementing and a strong working relationship with the users of the system being implemented. This person is generally in some sort of a business analyst role.

- **Testing** – Related to the bullet above – I need people who understand the business and know how to assess if the new solution is going to improve on the old.

- **Technical skills** – Generally the critical path skill on a project. Assess what you need – is it database, programming, integration work? Assess up front and get people who are good at it. If you don't have these skills get them from your vendor or hire consultants to assist.

- **Proven technology people** – I'm assuming that there is a development or integration component to your project.

- **Experienced vendor resources** – When you are implementing a vendor solution, you will likely have resources from the vendor working as part of the team. I find it interesting that when a firm hires a full-time employee, they generally have a comprehensive vetting process that involves interviews, references, etc. However, with vendor resources, they typically take whoever is assigned by the vendor. This is a mistake. All vendor resources are not created equal – some are great and some are inexperienced and not so great. Treat vendor resources with the same care you would when selecting full-time employees and ask the vendor for options – you generally won't get options unless you ask for them. Also, don't be afraid to ask for references on the vendor's resources. Ask to speak with a client who has had them on the team recently to get a sense of their strength and performance. If a vendor cannot provide you adequate resources, you can potentially get better candidates by contracting with a third-party consulting firm.

Unfortunately, this is not what the team often looks like. Put the effort in to get the right team – it is critically important.

If I could pick only one success factor in getting your project to a happy place, it would be getting a talented team with the necessary skills to get the job done.

Self-Reflection – On the A-Team or the B-Team?

Every place I have ever worked has had an A-team and a B-team. You are never told which team you are on but a little self-evaluation can help you figure it out pretty easily. I'm sure there are plenty of people who realize or suspect they are B-teamers and are ok with being there. If that is you then that is fine but understand the risks that go along with this designation: Lower raises and/or bonus, first to go during layoffs, less interesting work. There is also a pool of people who would answer that, obviously, they are an A-teamer but in reality, they are a B – these are the people I'm writing this for. Here is my breakdown of the attributes that differentiate the A-teamers from everyone else.

It's important to point out that there are two elements that establish your place in the overall scheme of things: Talent and Effort. Let's assume talent for the most part cannot be controlled – you were given a certain amount in some areas and less so in others. Effort on the other hand is completely in your control and if you want to improve in an area that you lack talent then you are going to have to rely on effort.

- **Source of answers or source of questions** – Are you someone who others go to for answers or advice on how to accomplish something or is it the other way around? A-teamers may ask a lot of questions but they are sought out because of their knowledge and expertise.

- **Waiting on others or enabling others** – 'I'm waiting to hear back from …', 'I need someone to help me with…', 'I have never been trained on that …' – these are B-team answers.

- **Master of domain(s)** – Are you the best, most knowledgeable, or considered an expert on anything in your job or role? B-teamers answer 'no'.

- **Playground test** – Your group or team is standing on the playground like when we were kids. Two leaders start picking their players – when do you get picked?

- **Highway test** – You are a car and you are on the highway – are you passing or getting passed? Example: I have worked in my role for 2 years but I find that the person hired 6 months ago seems to know more every month and probably knows it better than I do.

- **Objective facts not excuses** - What does your body of work tell you – Effort is important but does it create results?

    - Sales – How much business did I close?

    - Project manager – Were the last few projects I managed on time and budget?

    - Consultant – Would client give great reference on the work I just did for them over last 6 months?

B-teamers often play a valuable role but they are not the A-team. If you are a B-teamer and that is where you want to be, then that is cool – just be the best you can be. Determine where you fit and where you want to be and then decide if you need to take action to change your situation.

What's the Plan? Give Me a Practical Tracking Mechanism

I don't care what tool you use for project planning: Excel, MS Project, or some other option – as someone sponsoring a project, I want to see the following things and I want it tracked on a periodic basis:

- **Work breakdown structure** – I want to be able to visualize the components of the project and how the problem is being approached from an overall standpoint. What are the subprojects and who is responsible for them? I want deadlines but it is important that the resources working on the project have input and are owning those deadlines.

- **Milestones** – Give me meaningful milestones that demonstrate completion of something deliverable, measurable, and shows progress in the process. Along with the dates, I should know if I am tracking on my budget – this part is often overlooked. If I've got 20% of the work done but 50% of budget burned, I know I'm going to be in trouble if I don't do something to get back on track – the longer you wait, the harder it is to recover.

- **Visualize schedule slippage and make users accountable to their deadlines** – This is easier said than done. Clients will blame the vendor and the vendor will say they are not getting what they need from the client. The truth is often in the middle.

- **Create a project culture that does not accept waiting as an excuse** – A good project manager cuts through this and eliminates the bottleneck. How many times in a status meeting have you heard 'I sent them a question on this and have not heard back so I can't do anything further'? The reality is that people are often perfectly happy to keep waiting because it is off their plate and they can work on other things while claiming the slippage is not their fault.

- **Ask the senior sponsor of your project to randomly attend some of your status meetings** – Team members are comfortable telling others on the team about delays but they don't like fessing up when it is perceived to be career impacting. Watch how accountability starts to matter more.

My attitude towards project tracking has changed over the years. Tracking a project demonstrates you care about the schedule (and budget) and more importantly, provides a tool to enforce accountability. A few additional thoughts on your plan:

- Show me something – I want to see it. I don't want to just hear in a status meeting that something is on track or that it is done – I want to see it. Some things such as screens or a specific workflow are easy to 'see' while non-visual code or process may be more difficult to visualize. Either way I want to see something. I think it is good for the person responsible for the task because they need to demonstrate instead of just talking about progress.

- Long duration tasks should be broken up – make tasks smaller. If you say it is going to take a month to accomplish something, I will ask you to break it into roughly one-week chunks and ask what you are going to show me for each of those chunks. I want to see progress for the reasons mentioned above but as importantly, I want to see if you are on the right track so I can adjust on week one instead of realizing on week four that we have a problem. And the problem may not be the person's fault – maybe the spec was unclear, maybe a conversion was misinterpreted – it doesn't really matter (in my office they always just blamed me). If there is an issue, I want to find out as soon as possible.

Move Risk to the Front of the Plan

When implementing software, you need to consider the key risk elements of the project and have a plan for eliminating or significantly minimizing that risk. But this doesn't happen on a lot of projects – instead the risky things are often some of the more complex items so they are parked in the bucket of 'being analyzed'. This makes some sense in that it allows people to work on easily accomplished tasks and people can show progress right off the bat. The problem is that the risks still exist and the later you get into your project plan, the less time you have to recover if there is an issue.

Remember also that you have an acceptance/warranty period – don't you want to expose potential issues before this time elapses? Again – seems logical but many firms don't capitalize on this opportunity.

🏃 Project Managers Disappoint (But Some Are Awesome!)

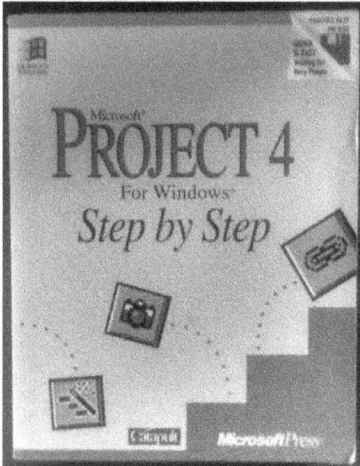

Actual Project Book that started my Software career. Note top right corner – comes with a floppy disk!

My first job out of graduate school was as a 'project planner' for a small software company. I read the job description and realized it had a bunch of project management requirements and expertise with Microsoft Project (project planning software). I knew nothing about Microsoft Project but wanted the job so I went to the bookstore and bought Microsoft Project 4 – Step by Step[19]. I read the book and learned about Gantt charts, start to finish dependencies, milestones, and the ever-important resource-leveling feature. I went to the interview and gushed my new collection of project planning vocabulary and got the job.

I start work and think that I have a pretty cool job. I'm a young guy and I'm in charge of managing the release schedule for the firm's software. I set up meetings and talk with people about progress, I update my project plan, level resources and deliver the bad news that we are 'slipping' on the schedule. Wow – do I bring a lot to the party!

One week, I walk over to one of the head developers on the team and ask him what percent he thinks is complete on the task he is working on. He looks at me with complete distain and says: 'I have no idea what percent I am at and I don't really give a #$#@ so just make up whatever is good for your plan and leave me alone'. It was a little less polite than that but you get the idea. It was a career changing moment in my life – really – a big one. That guy was absolutely right – I was doing nothing to help get to the finish line – all I did was bother people who were doing the real work trying to get to the finish line. Like Spaulding in Caddyshack[20] asking, 'Can I have your fat', I was just not contributing in a positive way. Maybe a better analogy is being the punter on a football team – you know they need you for a specific task but you really aren't considered a real football player. Watershed moment in my career – I was pretty upset and it was a key moment when I decided that I was going to have real skills.

I have worked with a lot of bad project managers over the years. The worst ones have the following traits:

- Ego – They think they are in charge and bother those working on a project instead of helping them.

- Admin – They like setting up meetings and sending lots of emails that make others less efficient.

- Lack Knowledge – They don't feel it is important for them to get into any details and have understanding of the project.

I had complete distain for project managers for years because I worked with a lot of bad ones and just assumed that was the role until I met a really good one. Here is what he did that made him awesome:

- He asked team members what he could do to help them. He facilitated communication across the team to eliminate roadblocks and built consensus on how things would progress.

- He scheduled meetings, etc. but kept them short and set goals in the meeting. He would crack the whip when necessary if we had a deadline and would work to coordinate what needed to take place to get there.

- He documented things for us to help clarify for client and vendor alike.

- He knew the problem that we were trying to solve and learned the software we were working on as well as anyone on the team.

- He tested, gave productive feedback, and kept a positive attitude across the team.

Wow – I had never worked with this kind of project manager before – he had a profound impact on the success of the project. I've worked with other good ones since then but will still argue that 3 out of 4 are marginal to poor at the role – not very good odds. Be the awesome PM and prove me wrong.

Pad the Plan - Timeframes/Budgets

I have debated with myself on whether to include a discussion about padding. The fact that you are reading this means that it stayed in. To pad an estimate is to make the estimate longer to accommodate unexpected or unknown effort that may need to be performed on a task. Even though individual task estimates may have their own level of padding, most plans can benefit from some padding. The reasons are as follows:

- On complex projects, the number of problems that can push out a plan are encountered far more frequently than good things that can pull the project plan in.

- When setting expectations with project sponsors and users, you are better off to beat your numbers and be early than be late and over. Give yourself some pad. This padding doesn't have to be on the actual project plan – it can just be in your communications to management.

What is the right pad number? It depends on the uncertainty in the requirements, the complexity of the project, and the expertise of the team but I say from experience that 20% is a reasonable starting point. Remember – you don't have to use it and hopefully you don't, but experience says to be prepared for it.

Positive Senior Leadership

During a software implementation, there are lots of people involved and everyone may not be on board with the decision to go with the chosen solution. I'm ok with people disagreeing during the selection process, but the implementation team needs to move beyond their opinions and refocus on being successful with the project ahead. This leadership needs to come from the senior management of the project. It is naïve to think that scenarios such as below have not undermined a project:

- Technology – We wanted to build the software in-house. If this doesn't go well, then we may get our chance.

- Project Manager – I'm friends with the guys at the vendor we didn't choose. I'm not really interested in implementing this system.

As a leader, it is your responsibility to get everyone motivated and dedicated to the project and to keep them in that state of mind throughout. It is not uncommon for people working on a project to actually want that project to fail. It is your job to make sure that everyone understands that failure is not good for anyone. Things are not always going to go as planned and there are going to be setbacks.

Several years back, we were working with a partner firm and they assigned a project manager to the relationship. After working with this person for a few weeks, my staff told me that on several occasions she was not supportive and seemed to be undermining the partnership. I called her and talked it through. I told her about the feedback that I received and asked her if there was anything I could do to help or alleviate any problem situations. I explained that she was valuable to our relationship but if she could not work cooperatively with us that I would ask that she be removed from the team. I think she was surprised and maybe a little bit embarrassed by the conversation but she turned out to be a great asset and team player.

Sometimes people work in a negative culture and it is just a habit to be negative or judgmental – you need to change that. Talking to people individually in situations like this is generally highly effective. You often get honest feedback from people on the source of their frustration and more importantly, you have served them notice that their attitude is important. I'm not suggesting that every day is a day for cheerleading; there are times that it pays to be the heavy and hold people accountable but that still does not need to be negative. Make a positive attitude a habit and don't tolerate the alternative, which is sure to undermine the effectiveness of your team.

Be a Winner Early

Aside from moving risk forward, most projects will benefit from moving some sort of high demand or high visual impact functionality to the initial part of the plan. Work on getting this element done early in the process and demo it to your users. Your goal is to build positive momentum at the beginning of the process. It gets the users energized and involved and throws a bone to the project sponsors who don't want to wait forever to see the benefits of writing big checks.

🤝 We Nailed It! A Cautionary Tale

Several years back, our firm decided that it was time for a rebranding effort for the company and a redesign of our website. We were referred to a graphic design artist (we will call Gilbert) and we sat down with him for an initial discussion. He showed us his portfolio and we decided to hire him. We instructed him that we were open to new colors, fonts and design of the overall website. However, we did <u>not</u> want our logo (which was a fish) changed in any way. We asked that he come back with some ideas in the next two weeks so we could collaborate on what we thought would be best for our new look.

Gilbert left and said he would be back to us with some ideas. Two weeks passed and we didn't get anything – he said he was working on it but needed some more creative time. Close to a month later he called me all excited and proclaimed that he had 'Nailed It!' He was oozing excitement and so we asked him when we could sit down and he said he would be ready in about 10 days. I asked why so long and he said that gave him time to get his presentation together.   We said we didn't need a big presentation but he was adamant, so we agreed.

Gilbert shows up at our office with a big box. We go into the conference room and he pulls out the following:

- New business card

- New letterhead (page and envelope)

- Frosted class imprint example on plexiglass

- Approximately 20 storyboard panels to show bad logo ideas that he considered and then decided against

I'm not sure where to begin but here goes:

- He spent a month working on a new logo (which we specifically didn't want). He said that once we saw it we would be blown away and would want to change it. It was not good – it looked like a dead fish in a net.

- He needed the extra time to send out the logo to have the frosty etching done on the plexiglass.

- We didn't get options – we got exactly what he wanted to do, which was not what we wanted. I was shaking mad. He was dismissed.

Gilbert was talented, hardworking, and believed in what he was doing but it did not end well. If we had collaborated more and took risk out of the equation early on, I think things would have been very different and would have turned a failure into a success.

Create a Culture of Deadlines and Early User Involvement

How many projects have you worked on that kick off and for the first 25% of the project there is no urgency? At 50%, everyone says that things are tracking on schedule (probably not).   At 75%, a lot of stuff starts coming up that creates issues.   At 75% of the elapsed project schedule, you probably only have 40% of the project completed and you have burned 80% of the budget.   People are working nights and weekends to finish.

I've heard it said many times that the last 10% of a project is the hardest part.   The reason that this is the case is that the last 10% isn't 10% - it's probably more like 40%.   It is made up of all the things that were overlooked, require rework, and need to be modified because your users say it needs to be done differently.   How do you avoid this?

You avoid it by creating urgency and milestones early in the process and by getting your users signing off on the functions and capabilities as soon as possible. Plenty of firms have said, 'I don't want to get my users involved until everything is finalized because it will make us look bad if it is not ready to go.' Fair enough, but in my experience, the problem with this approach is that it assumes that you really understand what the users want – which is often untrue. So, you work hard to test everything and give to your users in what you think is a final state and they say that it is not what they want.

'How To Do It' Is as Important as 'What To Do'

Most firms do a pretty good job of figuring out the tasks that their users need to accomplish but where they get into trouble is that they fail to grasp the ways in which users want to accomplish those tasks. This general concept is often lumped into the terms 'workflow' or 'usability' and is typically under-addressed until the users kick and scream and say it needs to be changed – something that will impact your budget and delivery date at the end of the project. A few examples:

- A trade entry screen – The business analyst thinks it is easy to enter trades. Traders hate it because they say the mouse is too slow to use – they should be able to accomplish the task using only the keyboard.

- Reporting solution that allows all statements to be generated with a single click. User say it won't work because they need to hand generate each statement in a particular order and want a manual approach.

- Portfolio rebalancer that allows system to generate trades based on user-defined allocations. Users say it works great and then realize that bond trades need to use par value instead of market value to generate trades. System considered unusable unless it can use par.

Each of these examples was tested by an analyst and deemed ready for acceptance testing by the users. The mistake here is that the analyst assumed that the workflow that made sense to him was going to be the same as the workflow of the end users. Notice also that the differences were not conceptually very large however, each required software rework which equals delays and additional costs. Getting a clear and approved understanding of 'How to do it' before getting too far down the path eliminates surprises. Yes – you need to get users involved earlier in the process. If you fail to go there, you are exposing yourself to future surprises that you do not want.

📖 Glossary of Data/Integration Terms

SQL (pronounced S-Q-L or Sequel)

SQL stands for Structured Query Language and is a (mostly) standardized language for extracting data from an SQL compatible database. SQL databases typically store data relationally – which is an approach for reducing data repetition and allowing for the creation of data entities that relate to one another. You may also hear the term 'No SQL Database', which refers to databases that to do not adhere to the structured relational approach and are often used in modern software applications.

Outer Join

I had been working at my first software job for a few weeks and I hear these two guys talking about doing an 'outer join'. I go home at the end of the day and I specifically remember telling my wife that I work with a bunch of geeks. Well, many years later I am one of those guys and have used plenty of outer joins in my life. Join is a relational database term that focuses on associating two pieces of information or tables together. An outer join is a special join where even if the join value on one of the tables does not match with a value on the other table, you will show the data anyways. Still a little fuzzy? Find yourself an SQL book (or a free online tutorial) and learn basic SQL – it's fun and the fastest way that I can think of to make yourself more data aware and versatile.

Integration (Plumbing)

Integration is a general term that typically refers to the data exchange that occurs between different software systems. A few examples might be:

- An automated file sent from a medical office to an insurance company to provide data on client visits.

- A real-time communication from an investment trading system to the floor of the stock exchange to purchase or sell a stock.

- Automation of your cell phone usage so your provider has bandwidth data to know how much to bill you.

The analogy of 'data plumbing' is used to describe 'pipes that exist between different systems to allow for data sharing'. The technologies and approaches to data sharing can be very diverse but can all fall under the general term of integration.

Feed

As an integrator (see above), I may be responsible for writing a feed. A feed is a term for moving data from one system to another. A feed can be written in many different technologies and formats but a feed implies (at least to me) that the data exchange is automated.

ETL (Extract Transform Load)

ETL is a general data integration term that addresses three common steps that occur when moving data between software systems:

- Extract – Taking the data out of a source system.

- Transform – Changing the data as necessary to prepare it for the destination system. When transforming, the two major things you are addressing are a.) the layout or shape of the data, and b.) any changes to the data that are necessary before putting it in the new system. Example: Source system may use Y or N in a field to indicate if a contact is active but the destination system needs the field to say True or False. In this case, Y would be transformed to True and N would become False.

- Load – The process of putting the transformed data into the destination system.

Data Integration – Interfaces, Feeds, and APIs

Data integration is often an important part of a software implementation. The term integration covers a wide range of tasks but it primarily focuses on the tasks of moving data in and out of systems or sharing data across different systems. A simple example might be that you have two systems: a CRM for storing your customer relationship data and a bulk email solution for sending emails to clients. You don't want to maintain two lists in the separate systems – you want users to be maintained in the CRM and then the email system can utilize those contacts. How can this be done? From most simple to most advanced, these are your options:

- Manual download and upload of contacts – Many solutions have manual download and upload features that allow spreadsheets or delimited files to be loaded. This could likely be done by a non-technical user on a daily basis. Good, because it is easily done with no development but bad, because requires daily manual processing.

- Automated bulk feed – Many systems have features that allow the manual download/upload process to be automated between two systems. This approach may require some programming and a scheduling tool to allow the process to be executed automatically without user involvement. Good, because it automates the daily process but could require some development involvement.

- Real-time API integration – An increasingly large number of modern systems have APIs which allow programmers to integrate systems together. In our example, let's assume the CRM has an API that publishes any user changes as they occur. The email system could be programmed to subscribe to these changes and therefore get user changes on a real-time basis. Good, because systems are tightly integrated on real-time basis but potentially higher cost of integrating the two systems.

Admittedly, I have dramatically oversimplified the integration discussion but the core lesson is that integration is about moving or sharing data between systems. In the real world, we could be dealing with data flows between many different systems and disparate technologies making the integration requirements particularly challenging.

🤝 Bad Data: The High Blood Pressure of Software

The COO of a midsize investment firm once said to me, 'Everyone in the firm wants good data but nobody wants to take responsibility for making it good.' Such a basic statement, but so true in many shops. Some firms have great data but from my experience, most don't. Big firms generally have better data than smaller firms because they have more resources (dollars and the people to manage it) to commit but that is not always the case. Bad data is like the high blood pressure of software – the problems are not always apparent but over time, bad things are probably going to happen because of it.

Data is a pretty extensive topic that we are not going to get into too deeply. However, let's talk about some suggestions to start you down a positive path.

Good data requires a commitment of time and resources.

- Clarity on the information that is to be maintained and if it is maintained, then users can assume it is correct. Either maintain a data element or don't. If maintained, then make the data accurate and if not then remove it or make it clear it should not be used. Bad or incomplete data is misleading and will lead to errors.

- Metrics on negative business events due to wrong/inaccurate data. Track how bad data is impacting your business and quantify those impacts. Is it hard dollar loss, errors that undermine your client's confidence? To quantify these errors will clarify your need to avoid them.

- Tools to assist those responsible for exposing risk conditions. Are you actively looking to avoid negative events due to bad data or are you proactively looking to fix data before it manifests itself as a problem? There are tools to help you with this – make a commitment to use them.

Data quality should be at the beginning of your plan not the end.

I've worked on plenty of projects where the client says, 'Yeah – we need to clean that up – we will get to it'. Get to it first. Bad data creates testing problems, a lack of clarity on what data can be relied upon, and just makes the overall project more difficult. Do a data assessment before you start your project. I have worked with several clients where we recommended that they put an implementation project on hold until data issues can get worked out.

Bad data is like the high blood pressure of software – the problems are not always apparent but over time, bad things are probably going to happen because of it.

Speed Matters

Years ago, while working at a portfolio accounting vendor, I remember, during a management meeting, the director of development talking about the throughput of a new release. His quote was basically, *'The good news is that the nightly cycle (system processing that happens overnight) completed without errors. The bad news is that it took 30 hours to run and it needs to be run every night'.*

System performance is a real risk that comes up in a lot of projects and it is important to address in your overall plan. Performance issues generally manifest themselves in two ways:

- Batch processes take too long and don't fit in the overall production window.

- End users experience slowness, typically in a user interface.

Diagnosing speed issues is not in the scope of this book (thankfully) however, I've sat in many a meeting that focuses on whether the speed problem is a.) database, b.) network, and/or c.) memory/CPU. A few entertaining quotes on this:

- **Technology:** *We looked at the database, network, and CPU and everything looks good – there are no issues with any of them.* **User:** *That's fascinating but it's still hanging.*

- **Network Administrator:** *We published the network traffic peak and it was 3% of available bandwidth but we were told that it could still be a network issue so we installed gigabit switches and fiber so we are happy to say that the bandwidth usage is now .003%. Unfortunately (and predictably), the performance seems pretty much the same.*

- **Network Engineer:** (During a meeting to diagnose speed issues of an application): *Why are we even sitting here? – It is always a database issue – always!*

- **Vendor to Client:** *I need you to double the CPUs and memory on the server.* **Client:** *Ok, we made the change but it didn't make it any better.* **Vendor:** *Yeah – we found a threading bug in our code – that was the bottleneck. You are going to need a patch.*

Performance issues are a real concern, particularly for large clients or situations with many end-users. Up front, I would ask your vendor if they publish benchmark results and/or make hardware recommendations. Vendors generally do not like to recommend hardware as they don't want to be on the hook for saying that the system will run adequately on what they recommend. If they do make recommendations, it will typically be for a lot more resources than you really need as a bit of an insurance policy.

Some vendors will publish a benchmarking document showing typical server configurations based on specific scenarios that typical clients may match. These benchmarks are helpful to the client as they show different scenarios and are also helpful to the vendor because it helps distance themselves from a specific recommendation.

If you consider system performance to be a critical factor in your project, then add a benchmarking test to your overall plan. It does take time and resources to setup but if you consider it a risk, then address it as early as possible in the implementation cycle.

Why All the Talk About Moving Up Project Risk?

Risky parts of a project are those parts that could delay or even completely fail a project. There are two main reasons that identifying problems early on is important:

- The vendor may need time to fix – Let's say you find a problem with your software that does not have a reasonable workaround. The vendor says that they can fix it but it is going to take them a month to get you a release to address the problem. If you found this issue with three months to go before live date, then it should have little impact on your timelines – even if the patch is delivered with some delay in six weeks. But what if you find the issue two weeks before your live date? You just added a month of elapsed time to your project and you need to retest the solution so you now must add on that time and cost as well.

- Remember when Shrek[21] said that 'Ogres are like onions – they have layers'. Software is like that too – typically built in layers to facilitate reuse and flexibility. The implementation of your software is built upon these layers so if changes need to be made, how is that going to cascade through your implementation project? If you are early in the process, the layers are just being built and there is less dependency on them. As you get further down the process, it is going to be more disruptive, which translates into time and dollars lost.

The moral of the story is that most problems are more expensive to fix later in the project than they are early on. Find them early and save your team time and money.

Third-Party Consulting vs. Vendor Resources

You have decided to implement a software system and are going to need consulting services with expertise on the new system to help with the implementation. Should you go with the vendor's resources or should you consider consulting from a third-party?

I have experienced this both as the third-party consultant selling competing services and as the vendor competing against third-party consulting.

- Vendors generally don't like third-party consultants working on your project in their place. Some vendors will have in their agreements that third-party consultants cannot work on the project or only approved consultants can be used. This is all about a vendor keeping control of the implementation.

- If the vendor loses the consulting business, it becomes harder for them to establish a good working relationship with the client. The third-party consultant is now the 'trusted partner' and the client's dependency and relationship is more with that firm than the vendor. Vendors also make money on services and don't want to lose this revenue source.

- Vendors are concerned about being blamed for a failed implementation even if it is not their fault.

In the perfect world, there would probably be no need to work with a third-party consulting firm on an implementation but here is what is not perfect:

- Consulting rates – Vendor rates are generally higher – significantly higher. This creates arbitrage opportunities for third-party consultants.

- Skillsets – The skillsets of third-party consultants are often better than what you can receive from the vendor. And, as the consultants continue to do more implementations on the vendor's software, they get better and more educated on the product. Many of these resources are also former vendor employees or industry veterans so they often come with an impressive track record. Despite this – beware – plenty of consultants will try and sell you marginal people – it is up to you to vet them out.

- Vendors can have a backlog of implementations – they can't provide the services you need when you need them.

- Third-party consultant's loyalty is to the client not the vendor.

I remember a software vendor once referring to our consulting practice with great distain and calling it 'parasitic' (ouch!). Consultants thrive on vendors who are overpriced, provide sub-standard services, and have an ineffective client relationship model. I think third-party consultants play an important role in the free market, particularly if vendors enable them. For both the client and the vendor, there are a few areas that need particular focus if a third-party is introduced.

- Client/Vendor relationship – It is important that the client and the vendor have a strong working relationship – the third-party should not replace this. The client should be sensitive to this and work to not put the third-party between them and their vendor.

- Hybrid approach – Consider a consulting team that consists of both third-party and vendor resources. Some vendors will not accept this arrangement as they view it as enabling to the third-party and a future threat to their consulting business. The nice thing about this approach is that you get the positive benefits of both a vendor relationship and a third-party relationship.

🃏 Questing for the Perfect ...

There are certain menu items that I put in a category I will call 'Quest Foods'. What is a Quest Food? I'm not exactly sure how it ends up on the list but it is a food that I will continue to order over and over to try a restaurant's interpretation of the item with the goal of finding the perfect one.

Why am I talking about food again?

After talking about chicken wings (which are an obvious quest food), I started to think about other items that fall into the quest category. I'd be lying if I said this has anything to do with enterprise software but I'm a little tired of proof reading so I need a diversion.

To qualify as a quest food, some attributes that I think are important:

- You must like the item – no need to quest for something you don't like, but interestingly, it does not have to be one of your favorite things.
- The item needs to have significant variation in preparation and opportunity for the creator to use his imagination.
- It needs to be fairly easy to find on a menu.

Gazpacho

When I was a boy, soup was, by definition, hot. You had chicken noodle or beef barley and it came in a can. As I grew older, I would see cold soups on restaurant menus and think – 'That is dumb – who would order that?'. Then I had gazpacho. Gazpacho is a cold tomato-based soup that has a bunch of other vegetables in it as well. Made with native New England tomatoes in August, it is just unbelievably good – nectar of the vegetable gods. The fact that it can be interpreted in so many ways is what makes it a great quest food. Made with green tomatoes? Include watermelon? Smooth or chunky? Spicy? All great variations that make you want to keep looking for the ultimate version. Gazpacho is also a unique quest food in that it is super healthy. Not sure if I understand the optional dollop (what a great word) of crème fraiche that can be plopped in the middle of my soup but bring it on!

Caesar Salad

Caesar salad is just an obvious quest food. Served everywhere, tasty, and can be engineered in so many ways. It can be a small side salad or a whole meal.

- Lettuce – Big leaves or baby Romaine? Cut or left long? Regular or grilled (just weird)?
- Dressing – Oil based or creamy? Mixed in or on side?
- Anchovies (a must!) – Traditional brown or white? Whole or diced?
- Croutons – So many good kinds but must be homemade.
- Cheese – Grated, powdered, or best is the pan melted cheese cracker on top.

I won't argue that a Caesar salad is particularly healthy but it does allow you to tell your mom that you did eat some vegetables.

Mai Tai

Most folks do not consider a Mai Tai to be food (some do!) but I'm going to include it anyways. I grew up in the golden age of Polynesian restaurants when they had bridges, waterfalls, and super cool umbrella drinks served in crazy glasses. They have sort of gone the way of the drive-in theatre but there are still some classics around. As kids, we would read the drink menu and beg our parents to get a Suffering Bastard, Singapore Sling, or Zombie just so we could see what the glass looked like up close. The Mai Tai was another drink on the list but it didn't have as cool a name. I'm not a big mixed drink guy, but it turns out that the Mai Tai is an epic cocktail. In recent years, it has been turned into a sweet blender concoction – I'm not talking about that version. I'm talking old school Mai Tai in a highball glass. An epic Mai Tai in Hawaii a few years ago made me a believer and now the quest is on for the perfect one.

Whatever you quest for, enjoy the quest. It's not about finding the perfect one – it's about experiencing all of them. Bring me a plate of wings, a bowl of gazpacho, and a Mai Tai to wash it all down – nice.

🚶 Good Juju: Ethics and Manners

I spend a fair amount of time out on my boat fishing. While on the water, I have run into many situations where other boats need fuel, need to be pulled off a sandbar, etc. Helping people makes you feel good but more importantly, I think it creates positive juju with the fish gods and that they will reward me sometime in the future for performing a good deed. I don't claim to be in line for sainthood, but I do try and let my ethical compass guide me both personally and professionally. It has surprised me over the years to run into some people whose compass was either completely lost or in need of repair. Below are some items that I have encountered that I consider at best unprofessional or inappropriate.

- **Employee poaching (Vendor/Client)** – Most vendor/client agreements have employee anti-poaching language. I think it is good for both parties to get some protection that their partner is not going to try and take their employees. I have had this violated on several occasions. Each time, the client says, 'We haven't made the person an offer because we wanted to talk with you first'. The damage is already done. The fact that you have already tampered with my employee and had the conversation with him is a problem. If I let him go, I lose the employee. If I make him stay, then he resents it and will likely go somewhere else. Not cool, regardless if it is the client or the vendor doing the poaching. If you feel you need to go down this path, talk to the other party before having any conversations with the employee.

- **Fly across country and cancel meeting** – Salespeople love to say that they are going to be in your city and that they would like to swing by for a meeting. Most of the time, they are in your city to meet with you and are specifically there to meet with you. Yes – they may have other meetings but trust me, they just as easily could have flown across the country specifically to meet with you. They also may be bringing their boss or an executive with them to impress you. Agree to meet with a vendor if you want to meet with them but emailing them two hours before the meeting and saying that you have a 'production issue' that will prevent you from meeting is pretty rough. Remember Marsha Brady from the Brady Bunch[22] saying to her date Charley, 'Something suddenly came up'? Bad advice from Greg Brady on this one.

- **Evaluating software with no intention of buying** – I saw a former colleague a few years ago who was working at a large bank. He said to me, 'We did you the favor of not evaluating your software because we were just looking at vendors to get ideas for building our own system.' I thanked him for not wasting our time but the whole conversation left a bad taste in my mouth. There are several 'buyers' in our industry who have the reputation of doing this. They are typically large shops who like to build their own stuff. They will invariably say, 'Management said that we need to purchase a vendor product for this' and then they go and do their own thing. A lot of the firms we deal with are very serious about signing non-disclosure agreements to protect their proprietary information but have no problem purposely wasting vendor time to learn how to build a system – a bit of a double standard.

- **Evaluating software for another vendor** – If you go through a vendor evaluation process, you are likely violating the NDA by sharing details about a particular vendor with one of their competitors. It is often that a person at a potential client is friends with someone at another vendor and provides this information to them. Another scenario is a 'consultant' who is doing a vendor search for a client who they will not disclose. They are collecting vendor information and will let you know if you make the cut.

What comes around goes around – embrace your moral compass.

Chapter 5: Going Live

You are reaching the point where it is time to cut over to your new system. Going live on new software can be stressful and disruptive to the business but there are some things that you can do to minimize this risk and make things go more smoothly.

Volumes and Application Type will Shape your Strategy

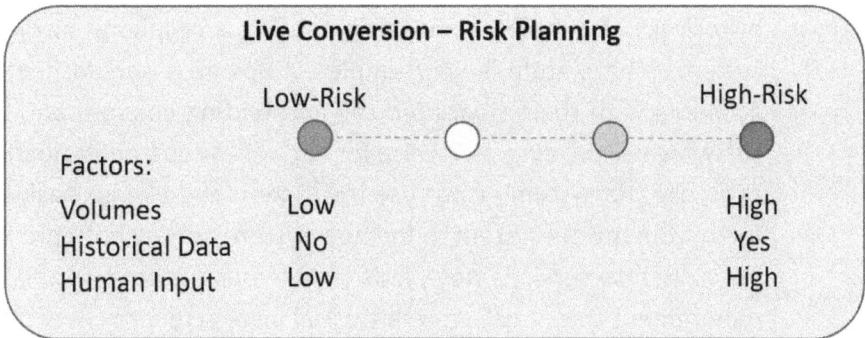

Live Conversion – Risk Planning

	Low-Risk			High-Risk
Factors:				
Volumes	Low			High
Historical Data	No			Yes
Human Input	Low			High

All go-live strategies are not the same. Having been involved in many system conversions, there are a few key attributes of the software being implemented that will have a high degree of influence on your approach.

- Volumes – High volume systems are harder to convert than low volume ones. What does volume mean? When I say volume, I mean the amount of manual entry, the amount of processes, the number of things manually done in the system, etc. Volumes are generally dictated by the size of the firm or how pervasively the software is used within an organization. Example: I have a new system for buying groceries. If I am I mom and pop convenience store, I do my ordering once a week and probably order less than 100 different items. I am in a low volume situation so there is less risk to my organization during go live. I can manually recover from any issues by calling in the order, email, etc. It is not what I want to do, but it is not going to paralyze my business.   On the other hand, if I am a large grocery chain, I likely place orders throughout the day for thousands of different products. My situation is different – as a high-volume user of software, I rely on it to help keep my business running smoothly and an interruption to this process cannot be recovered from manually. In this case, your conversion plan needs to take this risk into account.

- History – Does your system maintain historical data? If the answer is 'yes', then you have more to deal with than if the system is non-historical.   Example: I am implementing a cellphone invoicing system. The system is very simple – I upload a spreadsheet of accounts with their associated call and texting volumes and the software will produce an invoice for each of the customers loaded. I can use the system or not use the system and can go back and forth from my old system to the new system as they both provide me a discrete service. Now, let's change our system and add the requirement that it will store historical invoice records over time. This will make our conversion approach a little more challenging. Here's why:

  o I need to come up with a plan for loading the history from my old system into my new system.

  o What if I load data to my new system from the old system but I need to correct a mistake in the old system. Do I then need to reload the data in the new system?

  o Historical data makes you consider which system is the 'system of record' and makes it difficult for you to go back once you have converted over.

- Human Input – A system with a high level of human input influences your conversion plan. Humans generally don't like to enter data and they **definitely do not like** to enter duplicate data into two different systems. In our earlier grocery example, I'm guessing I could get the convenience store manager to enter duplicate orders once a week to make sure the new software is working properly but I'm pretty certain I cannot get the entire grocery chain to participate in a complete duplication of effort.

There are undoubtedly other factors that will impact your conversion process onto a new software system however, I think these three elements are consistently the critical factors in coming up with your plan.

Parallel/Acceptance Testing

Before we go live on our new solution, we want to feel good that it is going to work well for us. To accomplish this, parallel testing can provide a great dry run of the software without having to convert over to the new solution. Remember that this is not the first time you are testing the system. The implementation team has been unit testing and making sure that the component parts of the system are working as desired. The parallel test is meant to be the final dress rehearsal before we move towards the actual cutover to the new system. A parallel test normally consists of a test region of the new system being configured so that users can access and work with the system before it goes live. The benefits of parallel testing are many:

- Users are trained (or apply the training that they have already received) in a simulated environment to determine if they can effectively perform their functions.

- Individual workflow – Although it is preferable to address workflow issues before reaching the acceptance testing phase, it is typical for users to give their final review/approval of the workflow and usability of the system at this point. At this step in the process, users are forced to use the system and finalize workflows and therefore, are most engaged.

- Macro workflow – Unlike individual workflow which addresses the usability of individual people in the system, there is also a macro workflow coordination of data flows, timing, and all the events that make up the day in the life of the system.

- Calculation/Processing verification – Is the system working properly from end to end? Are you getting a full verification of results by comparing to the existing system or process?

- Feeds/Historical loads – Is the data in the new solution correct? You are verifying that the data is complete, accurate, and that the software written to handle these loads is working effectively.

- System performance – Is the system performing as expected? This may be your first chance to get many users on the system at once – now is the time to discover any load issues before you cut over to live.

From our large grocery chain example, let's come up with a general parallel plan:

- User involvement – We have established that it is unrealistic to have all orders entered in both the new and the existing systems so we have decided that each group will only enter their produce orders into both systems to limit the volumes that they need to dual enter. From these produce orders, we agree that we can reconcile this subset between systems to ensure that the orders are being executed properly.

- We will breakdown three parallel sessions and have each store participate in two of the three sessions.

- We will provide each store a file showing them the orders that they placed and require them to sign-off on the accuracy of the orders in the new system as well as agree that the system is performing adequately and meeting their specific needs.

We pick Wednesday as our parallel day as it is midweek and normally a day with low customer traffic so our order numbers will be lower and our users will be less busy.

Weds 1:

Things go ok. The stores enter their orders but have a few issues:

- New produce items are not showing up in the screen for the users to pick from – this was a minor issue that was fixed by the development team.

- Some training issues with the users – they were confused about the final confirmation process. We did a WebEx session for all the buyers showing them the input process and got some feedback from them on how it might flow better in the future.

- The feed that creates the master order file from all the stores is not displaying the expected purchase price. Not a show stopper item, but has been assigned to development team to research.

Weds 2:

Things go well – all items from last week have been resolved.

- One reported issue from an Iowa store is that the order entry screen is not working. Researched and determined that they were using a very old version of Internet Explorer – it was updated and issue resolved.

Weds 3:

Final dry run. Things seem to go smoothly – no reported issues and all teams have signed off that they processed their orders and they were confident that they could cut over to the new solution. All data flows have been reconciled and there are no known issues with the overall macro data/workflow process.

I will freely admit that this is a highly-simplified view of a parallel/acceptance process however, the core concepts of the process are reasonably complete:

- Users are comfortable

- System is performing as expected

- Data is accurate

Your job when building your parallel plan is to build out the acceptance and risk criteria that you need to test and verify before you are ready to cut over to the new solution.

Going Live: Big Bang vs. Incremental

In the spirit of continually trying to reduce risk, is it possible for you to incrementally go live on your new solution? To go incrementally live means that you can start using parts of the system and migrate on to the new system in steps. This approach is nice because it allows you to make a set of smaller conversions that are typically easier to deal with because they are less complex. The big bang approach means that you are going to cut over the entire system at once. Logic says that incremental is less risky and a better solution but unfortunately, there are some systems that do not convert incrementally very well. If you remember our matrix of conversion complexity, software that has high volume/historical requirements are often much more difficult to convert incrementally.

Think of ways that you can break up or stage your migration to the new solution. If you can come up with an approach without a lot of side effects, then it is normally worth going down that path, but sometimes big bang is the only logical approach.

🃏 Observations from a Career of Business Travel

I have been making notes for this book for a long time – the items below didn't seem to fit anywhere but I felt like I needed to get them off my chest, so here goes.

- **Why do New York delis always want to give you a bag and a napkin – for a soda** – I drink diet soda for breakfast (your coffee full of cream and croissant is no health picnic either so no lecture) – that is all that I would buy. The delis insist that I need a bag and a napkin. I have experimented in various delis across the city and the bag/napkin is pretty consistent – I do not get this in any other city – let me know if you have any ideas.

- **Open Mouth Chewers** – I would never have expected there to be so many see-fooders in the business world. You go to clients or prospects and they bring in lunch. Lots of open mouth chewers and not because they are talking – they are just chomping away with the doors open. And ladies, don't think it is just us barbarian men, girls too!

- **Putting on makeup while commuting** – I want to say I have seen a guy do this so I don't come across as sexist but that would be lying. I know you are running late but it sort of freaks me out – a little lipstick or something – I can deal with, but when you do the whole full face thing and pull out that Edward Scissorhands[23] contraption for crimping eyelashes, you have crossed the line.

- **Los Angeles**

    - **J-walking** – As a Bostonian, I boldly walk across any street in the city and do not feel contained to stay within those white crosswalks. No cars coming – I can go. In LA, people take this J-walking thing seriously. I was standing on the corner of Olive Street in downtown LA looking both ways before crossing and another guy in a suit says to me 'You better not go – I got a ticket here last week'. Just weird.

- o **Lack of downtown elevator warmth** – I'm not the most outgoing person, but when I step into an elevator and there is one other person in the elevator, I generally say 'hello'. This seems to be fine in most places and in the Midwest where the people are uber friendly, it is expected. Not in downtown LA – the people look at you like you are strange. I suspect it is because many of these people are soul-less vampires who eat too many avocado sandwiches. Be friendly in the elevator and we will know you are not one of them.

- o **Yoga classes walking in my back cast** – I normally bring a fly fishing rod wherever I travel if there is even a remote possibility that I can do a little casting. When going to Santa Monica, you can go right down to the beach and cast, which I have done on several occasions in the morning before heading to work. One problem – the yoga tribes that walk the beach at that time walk into your back cast – it is sort of amazing but it's as if I am not even there – stop it or I'm going to hook you!

- **Why does Cincinnati claim the chili mantle?** – It's not real chili – it is all soupy and strange. Chili should be chunky with beans. And why is the Cincinnati airport in Kentucky?

- **Philly Cheesesteak is overrated** – Let the hate mail commence but I have spent a fair amount of time in Philadelphia with different clients and everyone there wants to bring you to their best place. I say, 'I'm not really digging the Philly Cheese steak' and they say 'Oh, you just haven't been to the right place'. We go to their new place and it is sort of all the same – steak with cheese wiz on top. cheese wiz should not be on a sandwich. A steak sandwich is best with provolone cheese and mushrooms. I have an open mind – I am willing to take back this statement if someone can send me to a great non-wiz sandwich in Philly but until then I stick by my statement. I want to believe in the Philly Cheesesteak as much as the existence of Bigfoot, I just haven't seen the proof yet.

- **iPad restaurants** – This is a current airport phenomenon where you sit down and there is an iPad at your bar spot or at your table. You click through the menu and it is confusing and then you must click some strange order button that is not obvious and then you pay and close out your bill. What if I want something else? The waiter has to bring your food and drinks anyways – why not just take your order? They spend more time messing with the stupid iPad when they could just be asking me what I want. I don't understand the efficiency gains and I hope they all go out of business and get replaced by epic chicken wing restaurants with friendly servers.

Script and Practice Your Conversion

When it is time to go from your old system to your new one, it is called 'converting' and thus, you are performing a conversion. In all but the simplest conversions, there are many steps that need to take place in a particular order by different people. Sounds like a good place for a project plan that organizes these tasks and visualizes a timeline and approach for completing the process. Many projects have a project plan for the implementation process but do not have a separate plan for the conversion. The second issue with a conversion is the need to practice, or dry run, the conversion process. Why is this important? Several reasons:

- Practicing the process exposes tasks that were not necessarily on the first version of the plan.

- Provides real metrics on the time it will take for each task in the plan.

- A smooth conversion gives the end users confidence in the system. Let's agree that you are going to run into some issues but practicing your conversion process will help minimize them.

Does it take extra time and effort? Yes. Is it worth it? Your choice, but experience shows it makes a big difference.

How many times to do I need to practice? Practice until you get it right and you are confident that you have removed the risk in the process and feel good that the team understands their roles and responsibilities.

Work Together (In the Same Room)

In the current world of remote connectivity, the concept of working together is often accomplished virtually. My son plays with his friends but they are all sitting in their respective basements in front of their Xboxes with headsets on – this is considered perfectly normal social behavior now (even though it is odd).

When performing a software conversion, consider doing it the old-school way and get the key people to physically be in the same place (the office). You may say 'it is probably going to take place over the weekend so it is inconvenient for people and they have lives outside of work.' Yes – that is true and that is why you want them in the office. If you have scripted your plan, you get several benefits:

- You are not waiting on people – If everyone is remote you may get the message 'At my son's baseball game – will be home by 10am and can start my part then.' The schedule may have said that he can do it at 10am but what if you are running ahead of schedule – now you are waiting when you could have been making progress.

- Having people in the office will give you resources who can help with testing, troubleshoot issues, or buy pizza for the team. If these folks are not in the office, they will do only the tasks assigned to them.

- Working as a team in the same location is fun, it builds teamwork, and creates a comradery that will not exist remotely.

Consolidating the team is not always feasible but it definitely changes the dynamic of the process in a positive way.

What's Your Backup Plan?

Some conversions attempts fail. Even well thought out, practiced conversion plans can run into unanticipated problems that will require the conversion to be rescheduled. The challenge is that you may figure this out at step 90 in the process. If this is the case, you must have a plan for getting back to your old system/workflow without disruption to the business users. Sometimes this is very simple if a new system is being put up in a completely separate parallel environment but often it will require database restores, reconfiguration of user desktops, and a whole host of other tasks that need to be rolled back. The planning of your 'roll back' will help you schedule your conversion so that you can stop and reschedule efficiently and accurately.

Make your backup/rollback plan a key piece of your overall conversion process and if you are a project sponsor, ask your team what the backup plan entails. The business will forgive a postponement of a conversion but they will not forgive leaving them in a situation where they cannot perform their jobs.

You're Not Done On 'Live' Day: Some Bad Will Happen

Some conversions go off without a hitch but most don't. There are many reasons why problems are encountered and most are due to situations that were not (or could not) be simulated during your implementation process. Another key source of issues comes from the fact that this is the first time that your users are really using the software to perform their business function, so it may be the first time they are truly engaged with the system.

Let's agree that things will come up.

Like many support situations, some recommendations for dealing with the post-conversion process:

- Setting User Expectations – Talk to the users and explain that they are going to encounter some unexpected or problem situations and review with them the process for reporting these issues.

- Triage – You probably can't immediately address everything that comes up so build a list and assign severity and owners for the issues. Triage of items should be based on overall business impact or risk.

- Training – You probably did a bunch of user training during the implementation process. Users really learn when they are using the system in a live environment. Be prepared to re-train and support the users in this respect – often their issues are problems based on a lack of understanding on how to actually use the system.

Quantify Your Success – You Deserve It

An exercise that is often overlooked in the software implementation process is a quantification of the value of the new solution. Once converted to the new solution and given time for users to settle into it, spend some time putting together a short document that can be distributed to promote the success of the project. Things to consider are:

- Workflow efficiency improvements

- New functional capabilities they you previously could not do or needed to do manually

- Technology improvements that make you current and more supportable

- Speed/volume gains

- Strategic platform for rolling out additional capabilities for the business

Share this document/presentation with the project sponsor and senior management to help them understand the value of the project. You may think this is obvious to them but it isn't always the case. They have been writing checks and seeing the cost side of the project but have not been involved in the details so may have no idea of its real value. Help your company understand the benefits of their investment and congratulate your team on their accomplishment.

Post-Live Other Stuff

Settling In

You have the new system up and running and have gotten through the first few days and things seem to be getting smoother. Great – now we can start something new! Not just yet – keep settling in. Focus resources on optimizing workflows, continuing with training, and documenting processes and procedures that are in place. Just get things calmed down a bit and running smoothly. Then you are ready to start something new. I love building new stuff too, but make time to truly finish a project before calling it done.

System Upgrades

'I just converted 6 months ago, and now the vendor wants me to take a new release. This is going to cost me time and money and I really don't want to do it.' Fair enough. You can probably get away with skipping a release or two but as you keep pushing them out, you create the following:

- Support issues – Vendors get less effective at supporting older releases – they are best at supporting the current baseline.

- Cost of support – Many contracts state that only the last x number of major releases (two is typical) will be supported and beyond that all support is on a T&M basis.

- Patches - Most vendors will stop patching older releases. This means that you may not be able to get a fix if you stay on the old release too long.

- Incompatibility with other software – There are varying instances where older releases will not co-exist well with newer software. A prime example of this is browser support and the situation where an older version will not work on newer web browsers.

- Cost of upgrade – Waiting on upgrades and having to skip multiple versions will generally make your upgrade path more complex and require more testing.

The pragmatic answer on upgrades is that you can control your schedule but you should factor upgrades into your overall technology costs and strategy.

Transition from Implementation to Support

As your firm transitions into a live status, your support model will likely transition from that of an implementation team to that of a support team. Support teams are designed to support and triage client problems in a production environment. Engage with your vendor to learn about this transition and how you can make this migration as efficient as possible. Learn how to engage the support team most effectively and understand the vendor's knowledge transfer plan about your specific implementation.

🚚 Have a Great Relationship With Your Vendor

Isn't it the vendor's job to have good customer service and relationship management with their clients? Goodie baskets at holidays, swag for the troops, seafood tower for lunch?

Sure.

Some vendors are good at actively engaging with their clients and some really aren't. Regardless of their skills in this area, what is often overlooked are the steps that a client can take to foster a more beneficial relationship with their vendor.

- Who are your contacts? Foster relationships with different levels of the organization.

    o Executive – Do you have an executive level relationship that you can call on if something really needs attention. This is where your willingness to reference for the vendor can pay off.

    o Product Management – Do you know who makes the decisions on what gets put into new software releases? I want to know who is making those decisions and be friends with them. I want to be talking to them about my ideas so they find their way into future releases.

    o Support – Support folks can get beat up pretty good. Imagine if you took your core support folks to lunch and talked about how best to interface with them. You are always going to get support but I think you might see them a bit more engaged and responsive going forward.

- References – References are a great way to help a vendor but a better way to get some 'you owe me' points from the vendor in critical situations. I'm not suggesting that every client should be a reference. Make the vendor earn your reference as it is important that the reference is being provided by a satisfied and enthusiastic client.

- Collaborate – Collaborating on ideas is a great way to build a bridge between client and vendor. Regardless of the software system, it seems like I have always been fortunate to have several clients who were like software best friends. Building that level of trust and sharing is great for both parties and there is always room for more friendlies.

Chapter 6: Software Development

The first five chapters of the book have sequentially gone through topics associated with software selection, implementation and going-live. This chapter is different in that its goal is to help you understand some important aspects of software development with the intent of providing you a better understanding of how the process works and how you can apply that knowledge to working most effectively with a software development team.

Overview of the Development Cycle

(*singing*) 'I'm just a Bill, yes, I'm only a Bill, and I'm sitting up on Capitol Hill …' Schoolhouse Rock[24] is an educational, musical series that ran in the 70's/80's during the golden age of Saturday morning cartoons to teach you about all sorts of topics. Watch them with your kids – they are still fun and informative! The 'Bill' takes us through the whole cycle of becoming a law – very entertaining and educational. I don't have a jingle (or cartoons) but here is my significantly less fun description of how an idea ultimately ends up in the software you are using.

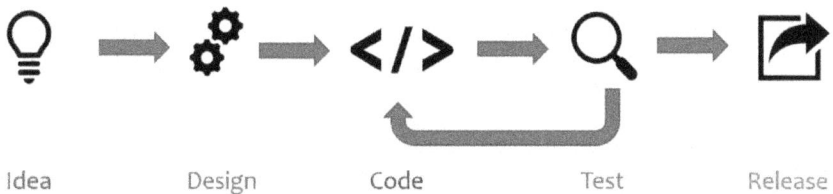

| Idea | Design | Code | Test | Release |

Idea – Ideas tend to originate from a client, the sales team, implementation team, or the product manager. The idea is vetted a bit and if worthy, gets put on an enhancements candidate list. You will learn later in the chapter about the process for getting promoted off the list.

Design – Once an idea gets picked, the product and/or development team is responsible for putting together an approach for how the idea would be implemented. This could include how to code, what screens will look like (if there are any), or changes to the existing interface.

Code – One or more programmers are assigned to write the code for the new feature. This is normally done in a development environment, which is a private place where the developers(s) can work without interfering/conflicting with other developers working on other projects.

Test – The QA or product team is responsible for unit testing of the new feature and for turning around bugs/defects back to the developers. The developer/tester cycle continues until things are working as expected and then on to regression testing. Regression testing is done once the new functionality is checked into a software release and the testers make sure it plays well with everything else in the new version. We talk about testing in more detail in the next chapter.

Release – Once all the new features are checked in, tested and signed off, the team determines that the release is client-ready and it is now available to be shipped to clients. Vendors may also release 'Beta' software to certain clients to help shake it out before fully distributing the release.

🤝 What Is Easier – Techie to Business or Business to Techie?

In the 1980's classic movie Trading Places[25], Randolph and Mortimer Duke bet $1 that Yale-educated money manager Winthorpe and street urchin Billy Ray Valentine can trade places given the right conditions. I haven't bet with anyone, but I have been experimenting with the concept of making technical people understand the business vs. business people understanding technology throughout my career. The basis for this experimentation was in my desire to have 'hybrid' employees capable of working on both sides of the equation. I worked hard to hire these hybrid types but they are tough to find, so I figured if I could build some of my own then that would be good for our business. My goal wasn't to make the business people hard-core programmers. I wanted them to have some database and scripting skills that would make them more versatile and better able to handle more of the data integration workload that the firm got paid good money to deal with.

After close to 20 years of empirical evidence, I draw the following general conclusions, understanding that there are definitely exceptions:

Business to Technical:

- Business people have the capacity to learn the technology but they decide it is not interesting and/or not imperative to their job success, and therefore, they generally don't commit to it.

- The business people who have successfully crossed over seem to be motivated by the ability to do things for themselves instead of having to wait for a technical person to help them.

- Business people are significantly freaked out by technology syntax. It just seems to frustrate them to no end so they give up.

Technical to Business:

- Developers don't have a great desire to become business domain experts but if it is your job to build something, you sort of have no choice but to understand what you are trying to build. For example, you build a bond calculation engine for an accounting system – you can't help but understand how bond cash flows work by the end of it. Suddenly, you have domain expertise in bonds.

- Most developers do not retain their business domain expertise because they don't think it is particularly important. Ask a developer in a job interview about the details of something he built and it is amazing how much they cannot recall.

Twenty years ago, I would have put my dollar bet on the business people – that they could cross over and become the hybrid skillset I was looking for. I figured it was obvious that a.) they could make more money, and b.) they would be more versatile and therefore, have better job opportunities.

Most of my experiments were largely failures but a few were not and those who crossed over have created a lot of opportunities for themselves.

Verdict:

Techies learn the business easier than business folks learn the technology. Techies have no choice but to learn what they are building and business folks generally don't perceive the value of having technical skills so they don't commit to it.

How Do Vendors Decide What to Build?

A vendor has constraints on the amount of time and money available to invest in a new software release. Let's assume that our development staff is fixed at 5 developers and we want to do a major release in 6 months. This means that we have (6 months x 4 weeks x 5 developers) 120 developer weeks available. We have vacations, holidays, etc., so we will go with an even 100 weeks available. I have several sources of ideas and wants that are jockeying to get on the development plan.

Sales-driven – The sales team is vocal about what they want the software to do. They are on the front line talking with prospects and being compared to other vendors and they want the software improved to allow them to sell more deals. As a product guy, I attended and presented a lot of product demos because I thought we got great ideas and feedback from talking with prospective clients. Prospects are typically responsible about not giving away the store on a competitor's capabilities (which I respect) but they will give you honest feedback when a competitor is stronger than you in certain areas.

Client-driven – Clients love to give feedback on how the software should be changed. These folks are working hands-on with your software so their feedback is often focused on usability and efficiency changes but they can also have great new functional ideas. One problem with client feedback is that once they supply it to you, they want to know when it is going to be completed. They assume that all ideas they report are good and that they are being put into a product calendar. Years ago, a firm I worked at had a software tracking system called 'the hopper' that was used to track client requests. It was sort of an internal joke when something was added to the hopper because it was like the chasm of ideas – nothing much ever made it back out.

Strategic – A vendor may want to build new software that increases their overall market or brings new capabilities or offerings to the firm. Development projects in this category are generally larger and require a significant commitment of resources so that commitment needs to be balanced against the demands of the existing business.

Given the above, I have a long list of development candidates. We have had some discussions about the different items and have asked the development manager to provide some high-level estimates on the development time to complete each item. We end up with a list of 50 distinct items with a total development time of 250 effort weeks. We are obviously not going to be able to get them all into the release, so how to pick:

- High-Risk Bugs/Deficiencies – If there are bugs or deficiencies that are forcing the support team to spend a lot of time in an area, this is a high priority candidate to be dealt with. Bug fixes are typically done in point releases as necessary but here I'm talking about larger items that need attention or are causing clients some pain.

- High-Value/ Low-Cost Items – Seems logical that something that gives us sales value and doesn't cost a lot of money to change should be on the plan. Marginal-value, high-cost items get put in the hopper.

- Client Consensus Items – When multiple clients are requesting similar changes, they get pushed higher on the list. First, you want to be able to say to the client, 'Look – we did this for you' and second, if these clients are all asking, it likely will help in the sales process as well.

- Client-Funded – If a client is willing to pay for a change to the system, it typically gets higher priority. Some have said that this is unfair and that funding should not be a way to move up in the priority list. I disagree. Clients ask for tons of stuff – we could never complete all the requests we get and many of them we would consider 'nice to haves'. If I tell a client that it will cost them $5k to get a change they want, and they say, 'I'm not paying anything for it' then my question is how valuable or time critical is it to get the change done? The standard answer is 'The software should do this'. Maybe true, but you are the only person asking for it and we don't consider it a valuable enhancement to the product. Different vendors have varying views on client funding of enhancements but most seem to embrace it as part of their overall planning model.

More on Client-Funded Enhancements

I have more to say about client-funded enhancements. I must be feeling guilty about asking clients to pay, so here goes:

- Cost Sharing – It is always nice to be able to generate some additional revenue but that is not the core motivation for charging clients for enhancements. If the enhancement was something that I liked for the product, I would often offer to split the cost of development. It became a cost covering exercise and gave me some extra incentive for building something that I was on the fence about.

- Client Engagement/Partnership – When a client is paying for functionality, they engage the vendor in the process. They work with you in greater detail on the requirements and want to be involved in the testing. It's sort of fun (most of the time) to do this and I think it builds a strong bond between the client and the vendor.

- Just because you will fund it doesn't mean we will do it – I don't want you to think that we would completely prostitute ourselves if someone is willing to pay. There were features and changes that clients wanted that we just wouldn't do because we felt it took the product in the overall wrong direction. Also, there isn't unlimited room for funded projects. There are other changes that we want/need to get into the software and typically less than 10% of the development calendar was funded.

Whether you love or hate the concept of client-funded enhancements, it is a way to move up in the development queue and I would argue is a healthy part of the overall development cycle as long as it does not get overused to the detriment of the overall client base.

Understanding Programmers

I'm going to discuss programmers a bit because I think they are a unique and often misunderstood bunch. I love working with programmers. Most are smart, passionate about what they do, and take pride in how things are done. Below are a few potentially unfair generalizations that will likely annoy some of my programmer friends, but here goes:

- There are programmers who continue to perpetuate the classic nerdy stereotype but it is becoming less prevalent, particularly with an increasing number of talented women joining the programming ranks.

- Programmers have big egos – Just because they aren't the loudest person in the room doesn't mean that they don't have strong opinions. Managing a bunch of software architects trying to agree on how to approach a problem is a challenge.

- Technical people think they are smarter than non-technical people. They understand things that non-developers do not and will use to their advantage. They will also purposely talk over your head.

- Programmers want to build things but probably more important to them is that they want to learn new things and new technologies. This is part of what makes them great at what they do, but remember that their learning goals may not be in line with the businesses' bottom line goals.

- Programmers love free food. When you are involved with the sales cycle you get used to lunch being brought in, but this doesn't trickle down to the development staff. Take a programmer to lunch (Chinese food seems to be a favorite) and make a friend for life.

Effort Inspires

I ran a company for well over a decade and I felt one of my most important jobs on a day to day basis was to keep people motivated and engaged and feeling like they were working towards an important goal. We all have good and bad days and some days it is just harder to bring the energy. One thing I always looked for was examples of effort that made me feel good. I had a handful of employees I could count on for this and it was a key character trait that made them special. It just charges your batteries and it's contagious. I've experienced this with employees and clients on numerous occasions but you can find examples everywhere. Two examples at opposite ends of the spectrum:

Do this:

Yard Work Laborer – I'm working on my yard with a landscape crew. The boss is there directing the job and several laborers are digging holes, hauling stuff, and basically doing a bunch of hard work in the hot sun. It's the end of the day and I have to leave for some reason – so the guys stay to finish the job. I get a text that night from one of the laborers (he got my number from his boss). He walked around the yard, picked up all my tools, lined them up under the porch to keep them dry and the text is to let me know where he left them. Splitting atoms? No, but effort inspires.

This example is the opposite – like anti-karma – don't do this:

Gas Station Attendant – I pull into a gas station that is full-service. I don't like full-service because it takes longer but some towns don't allow self-service (not sure why) so I get in line. Stick with me on this. There are two pumps with lanes on either side so four cars can be fueling at the same time (two on each side). I am at the second pump behind a car at the first pump. I turn my car off. Car in front of me finishes and drives off. Gas attendant picks up the gas nozzle from slot one, looks at me and shakes the nozzle. I translate this as 'If you want some gas you are going to have to drive to me because I'm not walking that 20 feet to your car'. What a raging ***hole but I'm about to run out of fuel so I pull up. I lower my window to tell him to fill it up but he won't come to my side of the car. He uses his finger to give me the 'roll down' the passenger window so I can speak to him without him having to move from where he is standing. I'm not sure if this story translates well but it really pissed me off. It wasn't about the stupid gas – it was about his anti-effort, choosing to be a loser. I ranted to my 8-year-old son the whole way home about being whatever you want in life but work hard at being good at it and passionate about it. I'm sure he wondered why I was yelling at him about the gas guy – probably felt he should have stayed home with his Xbox.

Leadership and inspiration don't have to come from the top – decide what side of the karma wall you want to hang out on and realize the positive influence you can have at any level in an organization.

Major and Minor Releases

Some quick thoughts on software releases. There are major releases, minor releases and sometimes releases that fall somewhere in the middle. You will see conventions such as Version 5.6.12, Version 6 - build 154, etc. – they are all ways of describing a specific version of the software.

There are terms such as Patch, Point and Maintenance Release to describe these releases. The problem is that everyone seems to have a slightly different definition of what each of these means. We are going to simplify and generalize so we have a basic understanding of what we are dealing with:

- Major Release – A release that likely has some large structural changes, major new features, or a fundamental change in the technology of the product. Expect that upgrading to a new major release will take some time and effort. If the first number in the release is changing (in example above from 5 to 6), then you can assume it is a major release.

- Minor Release – Minor releases are designed to address bug fixes and small changes to the software. Vendors can have significantly different interpretations of what it means to add something minor to a release but typically these changes are not having major impacts to the software and upgrading from one minor release to another should be much more straightforward than a major release upgrade. Maintenance releases, point releases, and service packs are generally minor releases. A patch release or hotfix may be generated to address a single or specific group of fixes.

The key thing to get out of this discussion is that there are releases that have a lot of change and others that have very little change. Ask the vendor to clarify their terminology and approach to understand how they handle the process.

New vs. Mature Vendors – Speed of Development/Testing

A co-worker once called me a 'cowboy coder'. I think it was meant as an insult (I don't think he liked me very much) but I refused to take it that way. First, cowboys are pretty cool and second, I think the person was alluding to my willingness to forsake a formal development process with the goal of getting functionality built faster. At the time, I was the product manager for a new product that we were trying to get some traction with in the marketplace. We needed capabilities and we needed them fast if we were going to start making some sales. I don't think this is unusual for new or emerging software products. Whether you think it is good or bad likely has to do with your risk tolerance and your willingness to accept some of the potential negative byproducts of an aggressive development cycle.

More mature companies and products get more conservative and for good reason: they have many clients using their software and have a responsibility to keep that software stable.

Immature vendors can be more aggressive with development because they have a culture to build, realize they die without more capabilities, and have less client risk. Several vendors that I have worked at in early stages would actually build software for a prospective client to win business. At the first demo, the prospect points out some shortcomings in our system but after a month of hard coding, we would go back for a follow-up demo with a new release designed to close that gap. Reckless development? Not to me – we built some great stuff in these situations.

The next time you say to your vendor, 'I just need a quick fix', whether you get it (and quickly) is often determined by the overall maturity of the vendor. This will be discussed a bit more in the next chapter as it relates to the testing cycle. We are going to dive into the concept of source control next as it is very closely related to this discussion.

Source Control – Why You Should Care

Most non-technical people don't care about (or have never heard of) the concept of source control. Many of you are thinking 'I do not want to read this – it is going to be boring'. I'm going to give you a rundown of what it is and why you need to at least care a little bit if you are involved with implementing software. I searched the web looking for a simple definition of source control (also referred to as version control or revision control) but they were a little too techie, so here is mine:

Source control is keeping track of the files and resources (source code) that make up the pieces of the software and the management of the changes to those files over time.

Not clear yet? Let's make a simple example:

Team project in college – writing a paper together.

Two other students and I have been grouped together as a team to write an essay called 'Our Favorite Animals'. We decide that each of us is going to write a paragraph on our favorite animal and when we are done we will **merge** the three documents into one master document and call that draft 1. We all look at draft 1 and decide it could use some editing. We each take a copy of draft 1 and make changes to it. Now we have three different **branches** of the document. We decide that my edits are the best so we are going to call that the **baseline** and add any other changes from the other two edits to my version and now we call this draft 2. We sit together and do some final wordsmithing, decide we are happy with the result and that is saved as draft 3, which we are going to promote to the final **release** to be shipped to the professor.

Now a software example:

- We build an application that consists of three text files (a,b,c).

- We compile the application into a build or release called version 1 and send it to you.

- You install the application and test it. It seems to work fine but one of the buttons is blue instead of red. You call the vendor and they say, 'that is going to require a new build'.

- Vendor changes file b (which sets the color of the button) and creates version 2 and sends it to you. A change was also made to make the button bigger.

- You test out and see that the button is now red but the button is now twice as big as it used to be. What happened? You call the vendor and they say that was an enhancement that was put into version 2.

- You hate the size of the button and are frustrated as to why you didn't just get the fix for the color. How did this happen?

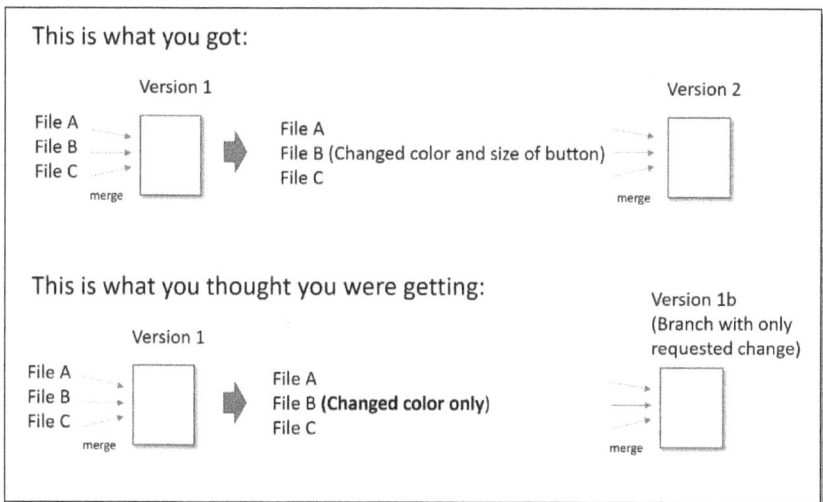

This is what you got:

Version 1

File A
File B
File C
merge

File A
File B (Changed color and size of button)
File C

Version 2

merge

This is what you thought you were getting:

Version 1

File A
File B
File C
merge

File A
File B (Changed color only)
File C

Version 1b
(Branch with only requested change)

merge

Software vendors generally want you to be on a standard baseline of code. A standard baseline is typically a collection of code that is tested and released in a periodic cycle. This is generally a good thing for both vendor and client because it creates a common path that all the vendor's clients can work from. But from our simple example above, there may be unexpected consequences to accepting to move along the baseline because the baseline is potentially receiving many changes as it progresses. If you are 'taking a new release', be clear on what you are getting:

- Patch – Often does not require a full install – Typically a file(s) is updated in the software to fix a problem – normally for smaller changes. Depending on your definition, a patch can be a branch or a baseline release.

- Branch – A copy of your existing release that gets changes applied to it – this is good from the standpoint that the amount of change is limited to your specific need but potentially bad as you are now off the community baseline release. You are now sort of a software orphan. You need to have a plan to get back on to the baseline. Some vendors will branch, others will not, and many will claim they will not but do.

- Baseline Release – If you take a baseline release, that is good because you are on the vendor's standard code base that you assume is well tested and maintained. Ask the question though of how disruptive it will be to go from the current release to the new release. Are you going up one build or 50? How much change has occurred? Change can be good in the way of bug fixes, etc., but change, by definition, introduces risk and if you are close to going live, how much risk do you want to incur? Vendors will typically ship release notes so you can see what the changes are on each release. Can't find the release notes? Ask the vendor for them.

The concept of source control is typically managed by a source control application that is specifically designed to help programmers merge code, manage branches and baselines, and organize the overall process. My examples oversimplify the source code challenge as many vendors will likely have multiple production baselines and applications with hundreds or thousands of files to be managed.

My goal of discussing source control is to help non-technical folks understand the risks and consequences of working with different types of releases and the side effects that can occur with them. The next time you are getting a new version of software, you can now think about the nuances of that release and where it fits in the overall source control tree.

Building Open Systems – The Vendor Conflict

Vendors love to talk about how their systems are open, thus allowing clients to freely move data in and out of the system. The sales team will speak of their open database as well as APIs that make integration easier. They know that clients want to hear that the system is open so they emphasize the overall features of openness. The strange conflict for vendors is that they often really don't want you using these features and can be reluctant to assist or support you in this area:

Open Database

Many systems have an open database that can be queried and interacted with. Clients like this but it can cause problems for the vendor. Queries performed by the client can slow down the system performance of the vendor application. Clients can also 'write' data into the vendor database and cause corruption issues which can lead to downtime and unwanted costs.

APIs

During the sales cycle, you may hear a lot of talk about APIs and how they give access to business logic in the application. Often these APIs aren't really designed for public use or the vendor will tell you that they really weren't meant to be used that way.

Hosted Solutions

If a solution is hosted, the openness of the solution may be significantly reduced. You may not have access to databases or APIs and the reason is often that the vendor considers it a security risk. If you are in a hosted environment, be clear on what features are limited by the hosting and if this will impact your overall integration or production process.

Software Development Estimates – More Art Than Science

It is common for a client to ask a vendor for an estimate to build some new software or an enhancement to existing software. Vendors do estimates all the time, but there are several factors that make this common task challenging:

Incomplete information

When do you have enough information on a project to provide a reasonable estimate on how long (translate: how much) it is going to take to complete the project? Most estimators are working with high-level requirements when they put together a high-level estimate. Business people hate to hear the dreaded words 'it depends' when talking about an estimate, but it really does depend on the requirements and the details of what they want to accomplish. A good estimator is practiced at extracting key elements and requirements from a client but overall, most estimates are done on incomplete information. In this situation, an estimate is often padded but the pad is just a guess and as the requirements evolve, the pad gets taken up quickly. Also, I don't want to pad too much at this stage because I don't want to scare the client off if they think the estimate is unreasonable.

Chicken or Egg on Requirements Document

If estimates are done on incomplete information, then why not just wait until you have the full requirements done before estimating? Vendors don't want to incur the cost of doing a lot of analysis if they are not going to get paid for that work and most clients do not want to pay for a full analysis before getting a better estimate. The question is whether we need an estimate to get to the requirements doc or a requirements doc to get to the estimate. Clients typically want an initial estimate but once you have provided the estimate, they want to know why the estimate goes up. It went up because the requirements were more extensive than originally identified.

Designing for the Future

A vendor will often probe a buyer with questions about what they want to accomplish in the future and how they could see the requirements changing over time. They do this to help design how the software is built so it will be less intrusive to make future changes. Is it smart to build in some infrastructure now to make a change easy in the future? Of course, but it normally depends on whether the budget can accommodate it.

Who is Estimating vs. Who is Doing

An estimator is often a senior person who will estimate how long it would take them to perform the task. The problem is that the estimator will likely not be doing the coding and the skillset of the person who will be coding may force the task to be longer. Estimators will try to factor this in, but they often do not know who will actually be coding the project.

Estimate Limited to Coding

Estimators often focus on the effort required to code something but overlook the significant time it may take for analysis and testing of the project. A firm I worked at many years back had an approach where they would estimate the development only and then multiply it by 2 to get the full cost of the estimate. The rationale was that the analysis and testing effort combined was equal to the coding effort.

Tolerance for Pain/Budget Constraints

The estimator may not have the final say on the estimate. The vendor sales team may know about project budget constraints or have a psychological number that they want to be below ($95K is better than $100k) and therefore may 'fine tune' the estimate to fit their needs.

A Simple Estimating Example That Becomes Not So Simple

Let's use a non-programming example to try and drive home some of the concepts above. In our example, we are going to build a wooden box. The client wants an estimate before he agrees to have the box built.

Requirements discussion:

Client: I just need a simple wooden box that is 18 inches on all sides. My requirements are very simple.

Vendor: Seems simple enough – what are you going to use the box for?

Client: I'm going to sit or stand on the box – it needs to be sturdy and hold up to 250lbs.

Vendor: Ok, is there anything else I need to know about it? Do you want it painted, or is there anything else that you want it to do?

Client: No – my requirement is very simple – I just need a simple box.

Estimate:

Vendor analyzes the project and decides he needs:

- 1 sheet of plywood ($20)

- ¼ lb. of nails ($2)

- 1 hour of labor to cut wood and nail box together ($20/hour)

So, the total estimate is $42 for the box. Vendor calls the client and client agrees to the $42.

Vendor is driving to the store to pick up the materials and says to himself, 'I didn't ask if the box is going to be left outside – if so, I should use galvanized nails'.

Vendor calls the client and client says: 'Not only is the box going to be used outside but it may be submerged in salt water because I use the box on the beach when I am fishing.'

Vendor: I'm glad I called. I'm going to need to use marine grade plywood and galvanized nails so it is going to cost an extra $12 in materials.

Client: That is more than the original estimate. You can't still do it for the $42?

Vendor: if you are going to use it in the ocean, it is going to be $54. I actually have some galvanized nails in the shop so I can do it for $50 but honestly, I think you should go with stainless screws because they are the most corrosion-resistant and we can back them out easily if we ever need to get into the box. I can do the stainless for $60.

Client: I will do the $50 solution – there is no reason to ever take the box apart.

Vendor builds the box and delivers it to the client – exactly as he asked for it. Client uses the box for several weeks and calls vendor.

Client: Hi, box is working well but I'd like to make the top removeable so I can store equipment inside the box – this is easy to change, right?

Vendor – Well, it would have been easy to change if we had used the stainless screws but we didn't, so it is going to require me to drill out the top nails and then use screws for the new top – going to cost an extra 40 dollars.

I think I will stop the example here but a few observations:

- The carpenter will ask more questions the next time a client wants a new box – he is gaining experience at estimating this type of project and each time he does it, he gets better at anticipating the client's needs.

- The client provides the minimum amount of guidance with the goal of keeping it easy and keeping it cheap but in the long run he cost himself extra by not taking the vendor's suggestion of using the stainless screws.

The above example may be making you say, 'Perry is a vendor at heart – of course he is going to make the client look wrong in the example'. The irony is that I am making fun of myself. I was the 'client' for fifteen years, asking my developers to build functionality for me. I often didn't take my own advice because I had time and budget constraints. Developers would make me promise: 'I promise I will never make you change the software to make it do that'. A year later they make me re-remember my promise but I make them change it anyways.

🤝 Good vs. Great Software Developers

I have worked with a lot of different software developers over the years and regardless of the programming language or technology, I have always been amazed at the productivity difference between a proficient and a rock star developer. I'm not talking about a good one vs. a bad one. I'm talking about a good one vs. a REALLY good one.

My quick breakdown of good vs. great attributes:

Attribute	Good	Great
Domain Knowledge	Understands what he is working on but often doesn't strive to understand business and true purpose. Might respond 'it's all just code to me'.	Understands the business problem as well or sometimes better than an analyst working on the project. Fundamentally understands the business problem trying to be solved and can contribute to the overall design with creative ideas.
Architecture	Takes the requirements presented and codes a solution for those requirements.	Asks questions about the business requirements and how they could evolve over time and designs an approach that assumes change will occur and prepares in advance.
Code	Often codes in linear fashion and programs the solution but not necessarily organizing	Thinks about the problem and how it fits into the overall application. Architects

	for flexibility and reuse down the road.	for the bigger picture with focus on flexibility and future reuse.
Quality	Does some testing but generally relies on analyst or tester to tell him if it is done properly.	With clear understanding of what the requirements are, tests before turning over and takes pride in delivering tight solution the first time.

A few analogies:

- There are cooks and there are chefs

- There are those who can draw a nice picture and there are artists

- There are those who play guitar and there are crazy good musicians

I will talk a little more about the guitarist. I try hard to play the guitar. I consider myself not talented and the only way for me to become somewhat proficient is to practice and push through it – it does not come easy. I was in rural Vermont this summer at an informal bonfire and a friend of my brother's drives up on his ATV with an acoustic guitar in hand – he is off-the-hook good – better than I will ever dream of playing – I'm sure he has put in his hours but he just has gobs of God given talent.

I think this is true of many things: music, art – some people just have a special knack at things and it comes easy to them. I think software development is similar but I don't think people think of it the same way or can appreciate it because it is a pretty foreign concept. But for those in the software development space, here is my 25 years of empirical evidence fact:

A great software developer is 3 to 5 times better than a good one.

Let me break down my claim:

- Less time to develop

- You require less of my time because you understand what I want to accomplish

- Done right the first time

- Cohesive with the rest of the overall application

- Time is money

- Organized/maintainable code

So, if I had my choice to start writing a new software application would I take one great developer over 3, 4, maybe 5 good ones? – yes. Would I take 5 great guys over 15 good ones? I think I'd actually like 3 great guys and 6 good guys. Good guys are good because they come with a bit less baggage – they generally will do what is asked of them with minimal complaint. The great guys can be a little high maintenance and that needs to be managed:

- Want to work on new/interesting stuff and be the lead dog– building boring stuff they have done before can be left for the good guys. Think about asking Axl Rose from Guns N' Roses[26] to sing backup – just not going to happen.

- Generally, like to work alone and get frustrated by working with good guys.

- Architects – Great guys have strong opinions on how something should be done but all the great guys might not have the same opinion – plenty of egos in the room.

Bottom line - I want my team stacked with a core selection of great guys but also have some good guys in the mix to handle more straightforward tasks.

From a financial standpoint, great guys are a better value. A great guy will generally cost 1.5 to 2 times more than a good guy. But if we are saying that they are 3 times more productive on the low end then they are a great value relative to the good guy.

Throughout my career selling technical consulting services, I have always been challenged by clients saying: 'We can get resources for half the cost of what you charge'. I have worked with many of those resources and in the vast majority of situations, the high-cost, great guy would have been a relative bargain – not even a contest.

Chapter 7: Software Testing & Support

When you are using a software application, you probably don't think much about the testing (or lack of testing) that has gone into making it work until … well, until it doesn't work. A major part of the software development process is testing that the software works as designed, and continues to work as it is enhanced and modified. Testing is performed by a group normally called QA (Quality Assurance). The QA team is the Rodney Dangerfield[27] of the software development process – they get no respect. Everyone agrees that quality is important but when it comes down to salaries and influence within a software organization, QA is not the top spot. Not all QA teams are created equal. Some teams have great skills and knowledge of the software and play an integral role in the software development process. Other teams are much less effective.

In the previous chapter, we talked about the software development process and specifically the quality of the developers working on a product. I will argue that the quality of the developer has more impact on the overall quality of software than the quality of the QA team. Said a different way, you can get quality software with a great development team and a mediocre QA team but you are not going to get quality software with a mediocre development team and a great QA team. In recent years, development frameworks have become increasingly focused on building testing into the software development process and putting the onus on developers to test enable the software that they write.

It is important that a software vendor has a process for ensuring quality but it is also important that a client understands that they have their own testing responsibilities in the enterprise software process.

Vendor Testing

Vendors typically focus on two core types of testing: Unit Testing and Regression Testing. Unit testing focuses on a specific aspect or 'unit' of the software while regression testing focuses on comprehensive testing of the overall system.

Unit Testing

Let's say the following has taken place:

- Product Manager has put together a design spec on a new software feature that allows a spreadsheet to upload a list of contacts into the application. This feature requires development of a screen (so the user can specify the desired spreadsheet) and the underlying code that will parse the file and load into the application database.

- The developer codes the new feature in a development environment and notifies QA team that it is ready for testing.

What comes next?

It depends on the workflow and approach of the vendor, but a likely path is as follows:

- A QA team member is assigned to unit test the new feature. The first step in this process is to write a test plan.

- The test plan is designed to verify different scenarios, such as:

  - Can I upload a file as described in the design spec? Do the ten contacts I tried to load show up accurately in the application?

  - Can I load both .xls and .xlsx (old and new Excel formats) files?

- What happens if I try and load a non-Excel file such as a .pptx (PowerPoint) file? (negative testing)

- If there are 500,000 contacts in my file, will it load successfully? (volume testing)

These are just a few examples of what could be tested but provide an idea of the situations that the tester is trying to address before the feature is added to the system.

- The tester will work with the product manager to understand the desired outcomes and perform the tests.

- The tester will write up pass/fail scenarios on the tests and any failures will go back to the developer for rework.

- Developer fixes issues and tester re-runs tests. If all tests pass, then developer will check code into a software release baseline (see discussion on source control). If tests do not pass, developer will continue iterative process with tester until all tests pass.

In summary, the unit test was a focused set of tests performed around a specific capability within the system. Once satisfied that the feature works in an isolated environment, it is now time to move along and determine if this feature has had any adverse impacts on the overall system.

Regression Testing

Regression testing is designed to test a full software release to determine if the totality of the system is performing as expected. In our example above, we added a feature to the system, tested it, and then checked that change into the latest version of the software. We tested, what could go wrong?

- Improper files checked in – Developers can check in the wrong version of files that have been changed.

- A change to a feature breaks another feature – Modern code is modular and developers are encouraged to build re-useable features and functions. This is great from an efficiency and consistency standpoint but what if a common function needs to be changed? That change can impact how another aspect of the software operates.

To address these issues, we perform a set of regression tests. The regression test plan may be automated, manual, or combination of the two. The goal of the regression plan is to test a wide swath of functionality in the system to ensure that it continues to work as expected after changes have been made to the release. The regression test plan will grow and evolve over time as new features are added to the system.

If I am doing due diligence on a vendor, I will ask them the specifics about their regression testing process. It is an important part of the process for reducing risk for clients and provides some good insight into their overall software development philosophy.

Vendor Maturity and the Impact on Testing

We discussed earlier how the maturity of a vendor can impact their development patterns and a similar conversation can be had about testing. Immature vendors with less clients have less risk in pushing out new releases. They tend to be unit test focused and a top priority of the firm is to push new features and functionality to the marketplace to allow them to compete with the feature-rich mature vendors. They will generally ship releases faster and be more aggressive about getting their clients upgraded. The mature vendors have a different motivation. They will be more focused on regression testing and stability for their long list of clients. Shipping a bad release is far more expensive for a large client base than a small one. I'm not suggesting one is better than the other but buyers should be aware of how the different vendors are shipping software and the risk/reward associated with each model.

Client Testing

If a vendor does appropriate testing, doesn't it make sense that the client can assume the software will work and that no further testing is needed? In theory, yes, but there are several factors that make client testing an important part of the overall testing cycle.

- How well does your vendor test? Some vendors have higher quality than others – just a fact. Your testing is an insurance policy on the vendor's testing. Over time you will get a sense of how effective they are at shipping clean releases.

- How the software is implemented – Enterprise software is complicated, which creates a virtually unlimited set of scenarios of how the software can be used. The vendor does not test all of them. Testing how your firm uses the software is imperative as you likely have use cases that the vendor has never even considered.

- Unique use cases/less-used features – Vendors tend to focus their testing on how their software is typically used. If you are using the software like many other clients, then the vendor is likely covering many of your use scenarios. But what if your business is unique or you are using esoteric or less-known features? Expect that these items are tested less by the vendor and the ultimate responsibility of their dependability will fall towards the client.

- Integration – Vendors typically do not test software integration. They may test their feed and interface capabilities but they know nothing of the integration that has been done on your specific implementation. Even if an interface is vendor-built and supported – beware. If the interface is with another vendor it is difficult for different vendors to coordinate testing across their releases and compatibility across the versions can be an issue. The client knows their versions and is in the ultimate position to determine if the software is going to work.

Client testing is an important step when any new software release is taken from a vendor and having a testing plan and infrastructure in place to accommodate is a key element to ensuring confidence in rolling out to your end-users.

Recreating the Problem

Let's say you are doing some testing and you find an issue with the software. You say, 'this is a bug' and email it to the vendor's support team. The email you send is, 'I click on the save screen to add a contact and it blows up'. I know, you are frustrated that the software release you have been waiting for doesn't work. The support rep knows what release you are on so he pulls up the same version and tries saving a contact and it works fine. He says the dreaded words, 'It works fine on my machine'.

Now let's approach the problem a little differently. You are doing your testing and you find the same error above. You do some additional testing and try and isolate the specific scenario that is causing the problem. You send an email to support including the below screenshot and further findings.

To: Support

From: Client

Re: Version 4.4.2 release – Save error on contacts

Dear Support,

Below is a situation with the new release that is of high priority to our business. I am providing the error message as well as a screenshot of the specific data that is causing the problem. It appears that having an apostrophe in the client's name is causing the save error. Below is a screenshot of the error I receive in this situation. If I save without the apostrophe, it seems to work fine.

```
                                              Save   Cancel

    Contact Name:
    Susanne O'Connell


                    Error Message: Object Reference Not Found –
                    either field or value cannot be null
```

The point I am trying to make is that even though it is taking you a little more work to specifically define the issue you are having, it is going to help get the problem identified and addressed faster and more efficiently. The cardinal rule of bug fixing is that the problem must be re-creatable for a developer to be able to fix. The support rep now pulls up his version and tries adding a contact with an apostrophe and he gets the same result. Now he can say, 'Yup – I'm getting the same thing – let me get this assigned to a developer to get fixed'.

The example above may be a simple one, but it does exemplify the importance of helping the vendor isolate the problem. Scenarios can be much more complicated and much more difficult to identify the root cause but the work you can do to help identify will go a long way towards getting resolved.

The cardinal rule of bug fixing is that the problem must be re-creatable for a developer to be able to fix.

🃏 Not Exactly a Love Letter

Not too long ago, I was taking a trip from Boston. My wife dropped me at the airport even though she was feeling pretty crappy. I felt a little guilty leaving her but I guess not THAT guilty because I hopped right out of the car and headed for the gate. The next few hours were a bit odd so I wrote the below email with the goal of making her smile and feel a little better. I'm sure she would have preferred something with the classic romance of Jane Austin's Mr. Darcy[28] but this is the best I could muster. She signed off on inclusion in the book, so here it is:

_____

Airport security is just the worst – but not today. I went through in record time – omen of good things to come in my day.

I walk to the gate. Lots of wheel chairs lined up to get on the plane but not a problem – there are always wheelchairs going to south Florida and I don't have a job so it's not like I have anywhere I need to be.

I look right – there is a place to get a soda – I think I would like a soda. I pay. I look left.

It is a Kardashian look-alike girl; black jeans, knee high boots, white ruffled shirt covering an expansive chest area that I deem not natural. We will call her 'Kardi'. The jump out was not that the shirt was white and ruffled but that it was only half a shirt – the bottom part was missing – it just stopped below the bosom. Sort of like a football practice shirt - showing off the mid-section, I guess.

I get in line and wait for the wheel chairs to be loaded. The flight attendant guy with a polyester vest that is unfortunately tight waives me on and I go toward my seat – 19f (window).

I get to the row and I swear that Dougie from 'Life in Pieces'[29] is sitting in the aisle seat. I greet her with that warm 'Don't hurt me - hello' and ask if I can get to my window seat – she sizes me up, smiles, and lets me through.

So, I'm in the window, Dougie is in the aisle and then … Kardashian girl comes down the aisle and points exactly where I horrifyingly expect her to point – middle seat between us.

Dougie lets her in and she sits down and puts her expansive pink carryon under her seat. Then it starts moving – the bag. Of course – she has a dog – this is not shocking.

Dougie sort of freaks out. Dougie is allergic to dogs and needs to move. Call the flight attendant. Dougie can be moved, but only if someone will switch because the flight is completely full.

Enter – Vanilla Ice. Pale guy, flat brimmed hat sideways, designer hoodie – thinking: 'Hell yeah – I'm going to get me some of that craziness!'

Vanilla Ice switches with Dougie and sits down next to Kardi. They immediately start talking about the dog. She decides to take the dog out of the bag as we taxi down the runway.

I'm thinking 'This is weird' and then another dog head pops out of the dog bag – holy crap – there are two freakin' dogs! She takes white dog number one and puts it on Vanilla Ice's lap and takes out brown dog number two and puts on her own lap.

We are climbing to 10k feet and Vanilla and Kardi are chatting it up – I have my headphones on and am trying to ignore but it is just not possible – it is a combination of car wreck syndrome and Kardi's voice carving through my headphones, regardless of volume.

Attendant walks by – Kardi flags her down and orders a cheese platter for the dogs and two chardonnays for herself – they are not serving drinks yet but the attendant seems shaken and brings immediately.

The dog farts – it is pretty obvious. Kardi notices the atmospheric change, gives a little shrug, and pulls out the emergency procedure card from the seat pocket so she can start fanning the air like you would to start a fire – I believe she is trying to disburse the dog flatulence so all on the plane can enjoy. She fans for a good minute – what is the appropriate polite response to this?

Drink cart comes – more wine for Kardi – Vanilla gets some whiskey nips. Dogs are eating cheese – not really what they need at this point.

Things are starting to quiet down a little so I'm thinking that it is good time to eat my sandwich that I packed. I pull it out and dog one is glaring at me – he watches me eat my sandwich like it is the last food on earth – I eat my sandwich and look back at him with distain as if it is the last food on earth, thinking 'You ain't getting a bite you stupid little lap dog'. Dog rips a fresh one – I'm pretty certain he did on purpose to dull my taste buds.

Kardi is getting tired so she puts her head down on Vanilla's shoulder for a little nappy. Dogs continue to flatulate.

She awakens. States that the little white dog is shedding and starts raking though his hair – it is like a blizzard of white hair – my fleece sweatshirt is covered with white fuzz – there is fuzz everywhere.

Final approach. Touchdown. Kardi tells Vanilla that she feels like a 'zombie' and needs some freshening – time to get to the pool – thinking Vanilla can be pool boy. I think even Vanilla is ready to move on – this is not the Mr. Toad's Wild Ride[30] he was hoping for – he puts up his hoodie (it's 85 degrees outside) and pushes along.

This is all before I found the 2-foot iguana under the hood of my car!

I couldn't make this up.

The Last Word

You have made it to the end of the book (or maybe you couldn't take the torture and just flipped to the end). Either way, here is a quick summary of the most important things broken down into a few short bullets.

- Put the work in during the selection process to truly understand the problem that you are trying to solve and address both the functional and workflow components of the project.

- Get the best team possible. Skills are king – you cannot not make up for lack of skill with more resources.

- Build a strong relationship with your vendor. It is good for client, vendor, and makes things more fun.

- Move risks forward – It is often small missed things that cause issues at the end of an implementation cycle. At best, it will cause delay and at worst, could threaten the overall viability of the project.

- Bad data kills – Understand what data is fundamental to the success of your project and make a commitment to get it good and keep it good.

- Be mentally tough and positive. Things are going to go wrong – don't let a toxic attitude dictate the culture of the project. A final Star Wars[31] reference for my pal Ron: 'The Force is stronger than the Dark Side'.

References

[1] Konica Minolta Bizhub Television Commercial – When I Was Your Age, 2010

[2] J. R. R. Tolkien, The Hobbit. George Allen & Unwin, 1937

[3] George R. R. Martin, Game of Thrones. Bantam Spectra, 1996

[4] IBM Buzzword Bingo Television Commercial, 2007

[5] GAP Band. Album: Gap Band IV. Song: You Dropped a Bomb on Me, 1982

[6] Lotus 123 – Lotus Software (Acquired by IBM in 1995)

(Lotus 123 was the dominant spreadsheet software in the 1980's before Excel became the market leader and before your computer had a mouse!)

[7] John Gray, Men Are from Mars, Women Are from Venus: The Classic Guide to Understanding the Opposite Sex. HarperCollins, 1992

[8] Frank Zappa / Moon Unit Zappa. Album: Ship Arriving Too Late to Save a Drowning Witch, Song: Valley Girl, 1982

[9] WebEx, owned by Cisco, is a screen sharing/presentation application that many sales teams use for remote demos.

[10] Dale Carnegie, 1888-1955 was a leading writer and lecturer and author of the book How to Win Friends and Influence People

[11] Jerry McGuire, Directed by Cameron Crowe, Tristar Pictures, 1996

(Rod Tidwell is a colorful football player and Jerry's only client after he leaves his job to start his own sports agency.)

[12] Tommy Boy, Directed by Peter Segal, Paramount Pictures, 1995

[13] SpongeBob Squarepants Television Series. Created by Stephen Hillenburg, 1999-2017.

(Mr. Crabs is SpongeBob's boss and obsessed with money.)

[14] New Zealand Medical Journal – Flatulence on airplanes – just let it go. Hans C Pommergaard, Jakob Burcharth, Anders Fischer, William E G Thomas, Jacob Rosenberg, 2013

[15] The Wedding Singer, Directed by Frank Coraci, New Line Cinema, 1998

[16] Apollo 13, Directed by Ron Howard, Universal Pictures, 1995

[17] A-Team Television Series, Created by Frank Lupo and Stephen J. Cannell, 1983-1987

[18] CHiPs Television Series, Created by Rick Rosner, 1977-1983

[19] Microsoft Press, Microsoft 4 for Windows Step by Step, Catapult, Inc. 1994

[20] CaddyShack, Directed by Harold Ramis, Orion Pictures, 1980

[21] Shrek, Directed by Andrew Adamson and Vicky Jenson, DreamWorks Pictures, 2001

[22] Brady Bunch Television Series. Episode: "The Subject Was Noses". Created by Sherwood Schwartz. Episode written by Larry Rhine & Al Schwartz, 1973

[23] Edward Scissorhands, Directed by Tim Burton, 20th Century Fox, 1990

[24] Schoolhouse Rock. 'I'm Just a Bill'. Created by David McCall. Episode written by Dave Frishberg, McCaffrey & McCall, 1976

[25] Trading Places. Directed by John Landis, Paramount Pictures, 1983

[26] Guns N' Roses is a dominant rock band from the 80's and 90's and album Appetite for Destruction has to be considered in any list of all-time great rock albums.

[27] Rodney Dangerfield, 1921-2004. Comedian, actor famous for catch phrase 'I don't get no respect'.

[28] Jane Austen, <u>Pride and Prejudice</u>. T. Egerton, Whitehall, 1813

(Mr. Darcy is a main character in the book who, despite his wealth and good looks, botches it with Elizabeth Bennet. He works it out in the end though.)

[29] Life in Pieces. Television series created by Justin Adler, 2015-2017

[30] Mr. Toad's Wild Ride is an original ride at Disney World. It is a colorful/unpredictable ride that goes through the dark.

[31] Star Wars. Created by George Lucas. 20th Century Fox, 1977

www.ingramcontent.com/pod-product-compliance
Lightning Source LLC
Chambersburg PA
CBHW031932190326
41519CB00007B/505